D1585314

052948

THE HENLEY COLLEGE LIBRARY

FASHION UK

FASHION UK
CARYN FRANKLIN
WITH JULIET YASHAR

First published in 2002 by
Conran Octopus Limited
a part of Octopus Publishing Group
2–4 Heron Quays, London E14 4JP
Visit our website at www.conran-octopus.co.uk

To order please ring Conran Octopus Direct
on 01903 828503

British Library Cataloguing-in-Publication Data.
A catalogue record for this book is available from
the British Library.

ISBN: 1 84091 269 3

Publishing Director: Lorraine Dickey
Creative Director: Leslie Harrington
Senior Editor: Katey Day
Editorial Assistant: Sybella Marlow
Design: johnson banks
Picture Research Manager: Liz Boyd
Picture Research Assistant: Anne-Marie Hoines
Senior Production Controller: Kieran Connelly
Additional Research: Charlie Bird

Printed in China

conran
OCTOPUS

CONTENTS

FASHION TARGETS BREAST CANCER

Fashion Targets Breast Cancer was launched in 1994 in the USA. An initiative from The Council of Fashion Designers of America Foundation, it represents the fashion industry's collective response to the staggering statistic that one in nine women will develop breast cancer during her lifetime. Ralph Lauren assumed a leadership role in the breast cancer movement in 1989 in support of Nina Hyde – his colleague and friend and former fashion editor of the Washington Post – who subsequently died of the disease in 1990. Lauren inspired the national campaign, which was launched in 1994 at the White House by the then First Lady, Hillary Rodham Clinton, and was supported by the nation's leading retailers, fashion publications, models, photographers and the CFDA membership. The success of the campaign in America led Breakthrough Breast Cancer to negotiate the exclusive rights to run *Fashion Targets Breast Cancer* in the United Kingdom.

It is now a worldwide initiative. Currently there are active campaigns in Australia, Brazil, Canada, Greece, the United States of America and the UK. To date, nearly four million *Fashion Targets Breast Cancer* T-shirts, printed in various languages, have raised over $20 million for breast cancer research, education, screening and care.

Fashion Targets Breast Cancer (UK)

Inspired by the success of the American campaign, *Fashion Targets Breast Cancer* (UK) was launched in 1996. Based around the sale of the now famous 'Target' logo T-shirts, the campaign is now established as the leading fashion charity campaign in the UK.

Since then, over 200,000 T-shirts have been sold, helping to raise a staggering £3 million for the charity Breakthrough Breast Cancer. For the 2002 campaign, Breakthrough Breast Cancer hopes to sell 80,000 T-shirts – one for every woman who has died from breast cancer since the first UK campaign in 1996.

Ralph Lauren is Honorary Chair of the UK campaign and is joined on the Executive Committee by nearly fifty of the leading names from the British fashion industry. Fashion journalist and television presenter Caryn Franklin and fashion designer Amanda Wakeley both serve as Co-Chairs of the committee.

HRH The Prince of Wales is the acting Patron of *Fashion Targets Breast Cancer* (UK).

The campaign has unprecedented support from leading names in the British fashion industry, including celebrities, high-street retailers and companies, all of whom have united in an effort to raise public awareness of breast cancer as well as raising vital funds for research at the UK's first dedicated breast cancer research centre.

Avon Cosmetics, Breakthrough's long-term corporate partner, has been lead sponsor of *Fashion Targets Breast Cancer* (UK) since 1998. Since then, Avon has contributed £1.3 million through the sale of T-shirts and exclusive target-inspired accessories.

For further information on *Fashion Targets Breast Cancer* (UK) and how to order a T-shirt, visit www.fashiontargets.org.uk or phone 0870 3330322

With the valued support of

A V O N

partners for 10 years

INTRODUCTION

When you want a clothing store to deliver seasonal trends information, personal shopping advice and excellent treatment, where do you go?

And if you are still looking for a retailer who will buy with you in mind or ring up when something special comes in, then this guide listing 100 wonderful shops, offering service above and beyond the call is tailor made for you!

Each shop, accrued from a list of award winners and personal recommendations, has been visited before inclusion in this book. Since I believe that retail hospitality – from the initial warm welcome to the friendly garment advice, dispensed at the till, should come as standard, some shops, despite their glowing credentials did not make the grade. One well-known London venue was even visited twice before it was finally rejected. While other places that appeared to be so very intimidating from the outside redeemed themselves immediately, displaying staff attentiveness levels, way off the meter.

And this is the key to the book you have in your hand, for clothes buying requires a certain amount of emotional nakedness. More than a mere removal of garments in a cramped changing room, most of us invest the new clothes we try, with the ability to augment confidence or bolster self esteem. Clever independents know how potentially therapeutic any shopping trip can be and work hard to satisfy, training staff to know the product inside out and more importantly to understand the anxieties we bring as baggage to the dressing room mirror.

Being a privileged aficionado I have benefited from visiting designer friends in their studios, and helping myself to their sample rail, whilst having it explained in passionate detail – in the early days by John Richmond and later by Andrew and Ren at Pearce Fionda. And with my dressmaker Christine just a phone call away it was easy to adjust the fit. I want that experience to be available to all women who seek it. The shops listed here offer just such a service and more, and contrary to expectation are not aimed at moneyed clients – in fact if we got so much as a snifter of prejudice, the shop was dropped.

With approximately 1200 independent clothing retailers – 500 of them in London alone – choices had to be made. Some shops deliver high-octane glamour, others provide a traditional elegance. My aim in creating this book was to put all women in touch with a retailer who could act as a personal stylist and image mentor.

This is a book designed to empower you to choose a retailer who deserves your custom…it could be your ultimate style bible.

If you have any suggestions for shops that should be included in the next edition of *Fashion UK*, please email me at caryn.franklin@conran-octopus.co.uk

Caryn Franklin

Icons

These icons will enable you to see at a glance which products are stocked in each store and the specialist areas of each shop.

 Classic

 Contemporary

 Menswear

 Accessories

 Toiletries

 Home

 Gifts

 Café

 Store Card

 South-east England

 South-west England & Wales

 Midlands

 North England

 Scotland

 Northern Ireland

BARE DIVERSE BODY BASICS
YOUNG IDEAS CLUE SWANKY
EVA THE CROSS VANILLA TH
SADIE THE BRA LADY ATTICA
KOKON TO ZAI GEESE L'AMIC
ANANYA GARBO PUSSY GAL
BEAU MONDE RITA VALPIANI
THE WEST VILLAGE SEFTON
HERO BLUE LAGOON BOHO
MALAPA WARDROBE KATHE
GEESE SUNDAY BEST THE H
FOOTLIGHTS LYNX JANE YO
DULWICH TRADER CRUISE S

KTY SIX CARRIAGES AT THREE
1ODES THE CHANGING ROOM
HAMBLEDON KOKO BROWSE
HE GLASSHOUSE N. SHELLEY
PANACHE SHOPS FLANNELS
E SHOON GOTHAM ANGELS
ONCRETE VERDICT CORNICHE
TCHES RICHMOND CLASSICS
S POPPY INDIGO THE CROSS
E DRAISEY PAMPAS OYSTER
SE RELLIK MADELEINE ANNE
G WARDROBE JEANNE PETIT
ET DREAMS CAROLINE BLAIR

This chapter dominates the book because it includes the capital and surrounding home counties. The south-east of England is a notoriously wealthy region, renowned for its cosmopolitan status. And with London at the forefront of world fashion, attracting people from all over the globe, there is room for creative diversity and an eclectic range of shopping experiences.

It is truly inspirational that many of these eccentric boutiques can still thrive in a city where property prices and taxes are exorbitant. Independents in this part of the country do struggle, but by offering a niche experience, retailers have become specialists in an already specialised field.

The equally affluent neighbouring counties are also rich with exciting alternatives, with less competition and a huge customer base available – these stores offer a broad range of merchandise. There still remain many independents willing to take on department giants and high street chains. It is the excellence of the service offered together with a personalised selection of lifestyle goods that is the future of retail.

ANANYA

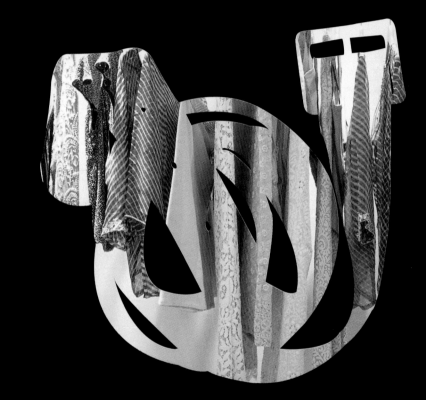

Ananya
4 Montpellier Street
London
SW7 1EZ
0207 584 8040
www.ananya.co.uk
Open: Mon – Sat 10 – 6

A two-minute stroll from Harrods will see you to the door of a magnificent, intimate designer-haven called Ananya. Wire faux shrubs decorate the exterior of this gleaming white boutique, where summer is never far away, whatever the season. The clothes, including Ananya's own-label range, are a colourful pot-pourri of exotica, energy and sex appeal.

Ananya's Bombay-born owner, Anu Mirchandani, originally studied interior design but moved into fashion design just two years ago. Her work moves fluidly between a diversity of ethnic traditions – from her native Indian to North African, Brazilian and Native American – combining colour, textures and design to concoct ultra-modern garments that encapsulate multiculturalism without falling into cliché.

The sumptuous Moroccan-style interior features a multitude of throws, pillows and other furnishings, many of which are for sale. The clothing ranges – encompassing not only Mirchandani's designs but a variety of hard-to-find labels from across the globe – are stunning must-haves that are are quickly snapped up by Ananya's glamorous clientele (Victoria Beckham, Lisa B, Roisin from Moloko and Claudia Schiffer are just a few of the names).

Mirchandani also designs and sells a magnificent range of jewellery, and plans to market a made-to-order collection, which will be manufactured in India using quality precious gems. There is a small but expanding menswear line.

Designs can be made to order, and appointments are readily made, either with Ananya manager Fabio Alternini or with Mirchandani herself, who works in the store as often as she can. Both have a natural flare for fashion and provide a genuine and enthusiastic service. One special extra is the reiki massage and colour-therapy treatments on offer downstairs.

ANNA

Anna
126 Regent's Park Road
Primrose Hill
London
NW1 8XL
020 7483 0411
Open: Mon–Sat 10–6
Sun 12–6

Market Place
Burnham Market
Kings Lynn
Norfolk
PE31 8HE
01328 730 325
Open: Mon–Sat 10–5

7 Guildhall Street
Bury St. Edmunds
Suffolk
IP33 1PR
01284 706 944
Open: Mon–Sat 9.30–5.30

Nestled amongst the candy-coloured shops and houses of Primrose Hill is Anna. This wonderfully elegant two-storey boutique is the London branch of a small independent chain. The other two branches are in rural Suffolk and Norfolk.

Behind the modest window display is a homely but uncluttered store; the layout is spacious and welcoming and wheel- and pushchairs can make their way freely. The ground floor is dedicated to the younger clientele, and the emphasis here is on daywear, accessories and lingerie as well as gifts such as jugs, candles and oils. The gentle ambience is enhanced by a seductive R&B soundtrack playing in the background. White-washed walls and pine flooring are given an original touch by the cartoon murals of girlie shopaholics that adorn the stairway. Upstairs is home to a more mature and expensive selection of garments by the likes of Maharishi and Eskandar.

The friendly staff, selected for their enthusiasm for fashion, encourage browsing and offer sound advice on styling and garment care. They're happy, too, to run up and down the stairs to kit you out as you luxuriate in one of the two good-sized fitting rooms. Private appointments can be requested, and customers are called with news of must-have acquisitions.

Store manager Natalie Goodman is on a first-name basis with ninety per cent of her clientele, which comprises young mothers, local businesswomen and mother-and-daughter combos. Under her management the shop has become increasingly more cutting-edge, contrasting with the two rural branches, where a more conservative outlook prevails. With a loyal following and its fair share of celebrity shoppers, Anna boasts a special relationship with local women. Whoever you are, however, you can expect specialist attention, as one shy thirteen-year-old looking for a bar mitzvah outfit recently learned during a two-hour marathon in the fitting room.

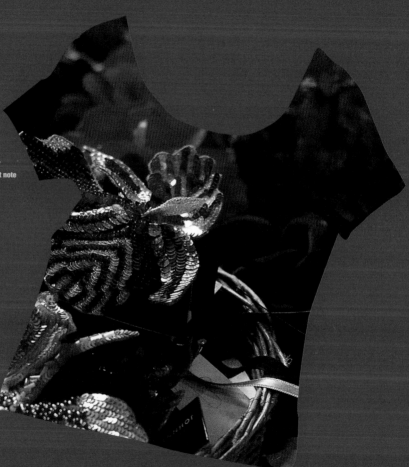

LABELS
Ann Louise Roswald
Cassandra Postema
Eskandar
Fake Genius
Maharishi
Orla Kiely
Rützou
Saltwater
Sara Burman
Velvet

ACCESSORIES
Adele
Victoria Fox

SIZES
8–16

RETURNS POLICY
No refunds; credit note
valid for 1 year

ANNE
FURBANK

Anne
Furbank

LABELS

Annette Gortz
Antonette
August Silks
Basler
Bianca
Catherina Hepfer
Cattiva
Delmod
Faber
Gerard Darel
Gerry Weber
Gil Bret
Gina Bacconi
Hammer
Kapalua
Kasper
Lucia
Luisa Cerano
Marcona
Michele
Olsen
Pola
Repeat
Sand
Tru
Vera Mont
Wille

SIZES
8 – 20

RETURNS POLICY
Credit note at
manager's discretion

Anne Furbank
41 High Street
Buckden
St. Neots
Cambridgeshire
PE19 5WZ
01480 811 333
www.annefurbank.com
Open: Mon – Sat 9.30 – 5.30

This upmarket quality store dominates the high street of the tiny Cambridgeshire town of Buckden, stretching end to end along one side in a series of Georgian red-brick shopfronts. The only other fashion retailer in the street is an exclusive lingerie boutique called Elouise, itself worth a visit if you're looking for something classically seductive. While it aims to cater for a broad spectrum of customers, Anne Furbank is proving increasingly popular with the more adventurous thirty-something and middle-aged women of the area.

Tasteful cream-and-burgundy signs mark each of the individual shopfronts, while the store's main entrance opens into an elegant reception area. Predominant throughout are wicker, ivory, beige and red, but each section of this two-storey maze has its own particular theme and style. In-store merchandizing plays an important role, while copious fresh flowers, elegant displays and spacious fitting rooms add charm and comfort. Extras include a slick Italian-style coffee bar and a play area for children.

Owner and principal buyer Anne Furbank moved into fashion retailing after working as a part-time model. She admits, though, to be having been very nervous about making the leap: 'I went into this venture completely green; it was all done on gut instinct. I remember feeling physically sick as I walked out of my first buying appointment, having spent £3,000 on clothes I just hoped I could sell.'

Twenty years on, with a £2-million turnover, Furbank gives much of the credit for her success to her staff, whose encouragement and enthusiasm have been a key factor in the growth of the business. She works wiith a large team of women – all chosen for personality and ebullience, rather than fashion or retail experience. Each is given training on a continuous basis, concerning product knowledge, garment care and styling technique, and over the years genuine friendships have developed between customers and staff.

The store aims to satisfy all fashion requirements, with departments devoted to evening- and occasionwear, accessories (including shoes, bags and belts), swimwear and perfumes. Additional customer services include complimentary alterations, an account card, out-of-hours appointments and, for recommended customers, a personal shopping system in which information is gained prior to the first visit.

Such are the charms of Anne Furbank that even a visit with the whole family in tow would not be out of the question – plan a day-trip now.

Bare
8 Chiltern Street
London
W1U 7PU
020 7486 7779
Open: Mon – Fri 10.30 – 6.30
Sat 11.30 – 6

A fresh new independent located off the Marylebone Road, Bare is owned by Tina Ferguson and Daisy Morrison. It offers a relaxing, fun shopping experience that could be likened to hanging out in a friend's house – if, that is, the friend happened to be well-heeled and blessed with impeccable taste in interior design.

The store has certainly been meticulously put together. Bleached wooden flooring and muted grey walls are complemented by two ornate fireplaces and gorgeous antique mirrors as well as various decorative touches that are for resale. The single spacious fitting room has its own fireplace, distressed golden walls and satin drapes, but the *pièce de résistance* is a 2m (6ft) painting of the Bare logo – a Fifties-style glamourpuss scantily clad in nothing more than a bathrobe.

Ferguson (a recent fashion graduate and designer of the Bare label) and Morrison (a former fashion PR and retail manager) are bursting with energy and enthusiasm. For all their youth (both are under twenty-five), the shop has been conceived and planned with consummate professionalism – and even the odd stroke of genius. Originally they aimed their buying at twenty-somethings, only later adjusting their direction when they

realized that their core clients were thirty-plus and also very diverse. Both Ferguson and Morrison have distinct personalities and tastes and often clash on likes and dislikes, so they established a buying manifesto: 'We go into showrooms with five women each in mind, and if the clothes don't suit these specific types, then we won't buy. They're like our imaginary muses.' It's a strategy that's worked perfectly so far, as a long list of celebrity clients, including Tara Newley, Nell McAndrew, Jemma Kidd and Britney Spears, proves.

Ferguson and Morrison quickly realized, too, that in order to succeed in the competitive fashion industry, they would have to offer some pretty unique services. One innovation is the evening parties where small groups of friends book an appointment to sip champagne, chat and shop in the comfort of Bare's lounge-style basement – complete with zebra-skin rug, comfy sofa and customized Bare table. It's proved to be a ground-breaking blend of socializing and accessorizing. Daytime services are just as exclusive. Ferguson will alter designs immediately, free of charge, and there is even a customizing service for clients' existing T-shirts and jeans. Both women dispense advice on colour and style.

Delicate, unusual design is at the heart of what Ferguson and Morrison do, so an expansion into lingerie (to be called Bare Necessities) seemed a natural thing for them to do and is in the pipeline. The sky's the limit for 'Bare's babes': 'We'd like to open another branch and then go global', they declare mischievously.

BASE

SIZES
BASE
16-28

Rushka Murganović   020 7240 8914

~55~

BASE
LARGE SIZES
16-28

www.base-fashions.co.uk

Base
55 Monmouth Street
Covent Garden
London
WC2H 9DG
020 7240 8914
www.base-fashions.co.uk
Open: Mon – Sat 10 – 6

Base opened at the heart of London's Covent Garden more than eighteen years ago. Its formidable owner, Rushka Murganovic, set up the store after identifying a gaping void in the market for quality pieces in larger sizes. She aims to provide quality innovative and sexy clothing for the fuller-figured woman.

Shopping in Base is an intimate and personal experience. The interior – a plush and welcoming cocoon with white wooden floorboards – is scattered with kilims and framed by walls painted deepest red. Clothes on display are free-flowing and often feature unusual fabrics. For Murganovic, buying is always a challenge due to the size range, but she tries to avoid all the predictable German brands and sources mainly from the Benelux countries and Sweden. Her love of Japanese cut and design is also apparent. 'I want to provide individual pieces that are unstructured and flattering to rounder figures', says Murganovic. At one time she designed and manufactured her own range, but with just one central store, her stock size proved too restricted to sustain this.

Service is attentive and chatty, and encompasses a genuine feel for the individuality of every customer. Murganovic works closely with Gloria Sinclair, a vivacious American member of her team who, as a larger woman herself, fully understands the stylistic requirements of the women who visit the shop. Although there is just one spacious fitting room, it rarely becomes congested, as Murganovic works methodically and is always available for private appointments. Alterations are a key part of the service at Base. There is a nominal charge – justified on the grounds of the guaranteed quality provided by the shop's long-standing tailor.

Customers travel across the globe to visit Base, and there is seemingly no age limit to the clientele. Murganovic says that customers range from twenty-five to seventy-five, and that designs therefore need to cover the full spectrum from 'classic' to 'young creative'. Asked what she thinks keeps her customers coming back for more, she replies, 'I truly believe that nobody does what I do. It's here in my head…how I see them.'

BERNARD

Bernard
4–6 High Street
Esher
Surrey
KT10 9RT
01372 464 604
www.bernardesher.co.uk
Open: Mon–Fri 9–5.30
Sat 9–6

Nestling in Esher's somewhat subdued high street is Bernard – a rather strangely named womenswear store that brings innovative fashion to comfortable, commuter-belt Surrey. The store thrives on the presence and personality of its owner, Helene Rapaport.

Rapaport has worked in fashion retail since the age of fifteen. She moved rather unhappily from shop to shop until her husband, Barry, encouraged her to set up her own business. Rapaport's first outlet was in an area populated by women of a certain age, whose conservative tastes left her longing to create a shop that reflected her own, more out-of-the-ordinary preferences. Finally, Rapaport took over a store in Esher that had hitherto been unsuccessful. 'In those days', she comments, 'you didn't even consider things like the area. If I had, I would have certainly opened up in Primrose Hill or Notting Hill Gate!'

The original aim was to call the shop The Course, but Rapaport finally opted for the name of an uncle's shop that she nostalgically associated with prestige and exclusivity. Although she says she now dislikes the name, her superstitious nature has so far prevented her from changing it. Today she and her husband run Bernard together. He deals with the day-to-day running of the store, while she focuses on the buying.

The window displays are both simple and eye-catching. Inside, grey and white shades form a subtle backdrop to the array of colourful, feminine and often flamboyant designs, cleverly accessorized with the latest belts, shoes and bags. Rapaport opts for an eclectic mix of must-have labels, with the focus on new designers, whom she often picks up well before their names hit the fashion news. 'I don't go out looking for certain brands like Gucci and Prada', she says. 'I actively search for unusual little labels…we are likened to a mini-Selfridges, but with a very select and different range.'

The staff, all of whom are under thirty, are friendly and approachable and have a reassuring air of sophisticated calm. The overall atmosphere is young and progressive – very much reflecting the spirit of its owner. 'I want everybody to love everything that I buy as much as I do…' she enthuses, 'I am very passionate about what I do.' Staying open late for personal appointments is a regular occurrence, and there's also (in addition to the four standard fitting rooms) an additional room for clients needing extra space or privacy. Bernard has a very loyal following among local women, many of whom like to think of the store as their little secret.

Boho
113a Northcote Road
London
SW11 6PW
020 7924 7295
www.boho-online.com
Open: Mon – Sat 11 – 6

South London's notoriously chic boutique Boho was launched by Johanna Pilgrim and Christine Roberts in 1999 and has been described as the shop 'perfect for the 21st-century deluxe hippie girl, who doesn't do hard tailoring and pinstripes'. Keen lovers of all things beautiful, Pilgrim and Roberts bring fresh, eclectic, feminine womenswear, jewellery, bags and accessories to Battersea's Northcote Road.

Surprisingly, the shop's location is a seriously revamped cab office, whose interior has been transformed into a compact, trinket-filled grotto with wooden floors and white walls. Jazz plays lazily in the background, adding to the general boudoir feel. Various girlie goodies are displayed on the Ikea Lack shelves that edge the walls; a distressed Victorian fireplace drips with jewellery. Even the pastel-pink walls in the fitting room at the rear of the shop are strung with fairy lights. Staff wrap purchases in fuchsia-pink tissue and deposit them in lilac carrier bags, all the while artfully dispensing garment-care advice and friendly conversation.

Pilgrim and Roberts are natural buyers, travelling all over the globe in the pursuit of novel acquisitions. New designers and current British names are mixed in with mouthwatering exotica. To keep things commercially viable, Pilgrim and Roberts select merchandize for its 'timeless quality' and buy in small quantities for an exclusive feel. A Kate Clarkson pale-pink satin skirt, beautiful printed fabrics in Tencel and cotton by the Spanish label Custo and a candy-coloured poodle-print PVC bag by Girl's Best Friend give an idea of the covetable discoveries to be made here.

The intimacy of Boho, together with its attentive, friendly and helpful staff, means that those who shop at Boho feel very special. The Boho loyalty card gives customers more of the same – for each £50 they spend they get a stamp, with twelve stamps entitling them to a £50 voucher that can be spent on anything in the shop. Private appointments are not necessary as staff will stay open late if needed for one-to-one consultations.

It's worth remembering that this special shop is also very small, especially if more than three shoppers happen to drop by at once, so it may be necessary to wait your turn outside. The wait, though, is worth it – once inside, you're bound to get your reward, so that even a bit of squashing between fellow shoppers will seem like no hardship at all.

CELIA LOE

Celia Loe
68 South Molton Street
London
W1K 5ST
020 7409 1627
Open: Mon – Sat 10 – 6.30
except Thurs 10 – 7.30

LABELS
Celia Loe

SIZES
8–14

RETURNS POLICY
Exchange or credit
note within 14 days
and with receipt

At the far end of London's South Molton Street is Celia Loe, a clothing specialist whose mission is to provide smart, elegant modern pieces for women under five foot five. A Singapore-based company, with a scattering of shops in south-east Asia, the company designs and manufactures all its own garments and is able to offer remarkably good value for money. The store's owner and chief designer is the eponymous Celia Loe.

Loe designs a broad range of dresses, suits and separates, focusing on elegant clothing that is fashion-aware but not trend-driven. The emphasis here is on working within the parameters of shapes and lines that will flatter smaller women. True petite clothing, Loe points out, consists of very specific tailoring, the crucial variables being arm and leg lengths and the relative waist proportions. These vital ratios, she says, are usually overlooked by high-street retailers, whose petite ranges often simply focus on shorter hemlines. Aware of the evolving needs of working women, Loe now carries smart separates in addition to casual, evening and core tailoring ranges.

The store is small and simple, with white walls and uncluttered merchandizing. The refined staff are extremely helpful and, of course, pay conscientious attention to fitting. As Loe notes: 'It's the person who wears the clothing, not the other way round!' The London store celebrates its tenth anniversary in 2003; let's hope that there will be many more.

THE CHANGING ROOM

The Changing Room
10a Gees Court
St. Christopher's Place
London
W1U 1JL
020 7408 1596
www.the-changingroom.com
Open: Mon – Sat 10.30 – 6.30
except Thurs 10.30 – 7.30

This little boutique is located just off fashionable Saint Christopher's Place and has successfully competed with the big boys on the block for over a decade. Credit for its prosperity is down to the justly celebrated service on offer. The creative styling here, using an exquisite selection of artistically designed clothes and jewellery, has people travelling from all over the globe for a visit. Owner and buyer Chris Moore works alongside manager and assistant buyer Maria Carla, who sums up the secret behind good service. 'Love people or forget it.' she says. 'Be patient and enjoy fashion. In this job you have to listen more than you talk and when you do speak, keep it short.'

The store carries an outstanding selection of contemporary garments for both day- and eveningwear. On offer are minimal fluid shapes combined with modern simplicity, ranging from soft and romantic to sharp-as-a-knife executive (some of the suits on offer look capable of negotiating a pay rise all by themselves). The Changing Room also features creative pieces by some of the world's best young jewellery designers, including names such as Satellite, Otazu and Delphine Nardin. Under Maria Carla's finely honed eye, such ingredients combine to create a bold individual look.

The store is appropriately named after its one and only changing room, although it is big enough to cater for a couple of close friends or even a party of three. Moore insists that there is no threat of an unsightly queue forming because usually only one or two customers can be found in the store at any one time. This allows for quality time with customers: just explain the look you desire, and within minutes pieces will be hand-picked from the rails and then complemented with accessories to create a stunning outfit for any occasion.

Alterations can be made to any purchase, including shortening sleeves and trouser lengths, and, of course, Maria Carla will keep the shop open after hours – an almost inevitable occurrence given the fact that time can fly by when you're in this particular 'Changing Room'.

CONCRETE

Concrete
35a Marshall Street
London
W1F 7EX
020 7434 4546
Open: Mon – Fri 10.30 – 6.30
Sat 11 – 6.30

Five years ago Phillip Stevens launched the fashion PR company Concrete, and now boasts a large number of prestigious avant-garde designers in his stable. It was always his intention, however, to open a store as part of his PR package – a dream he realized in 2001. Concrete, the shop, is tucked behind the rejuvenated Carnaby Street in Central London and has quickly become a cosy refuge for fashion diehards as well as a Mecca for the overseas tourists who swarm the district.

The exterior, sporting a black-gloss front and succinctly worded fascia ('Concrete Men Women Home') in plain white writing, is suggestive of somewhat run-of-the-mill designery goings-on, but once you're inside all such preconceptions are swiftly banished. Much thought but deliberately little sophistication has been put into the interior design, giving the store an enviable awkward cool. The hideous floral carpet is endearingly reminiscent of Granny's lounge, while a mannequin-and-glass coffee table – a prototype by Harris Tweed – firmly seals the tongue-in-cheek approach of this PR-propelled retailer.

Don't be put off by the intercom system; knowing that you may be lucky enough to encounter staff like Maurizio Bossetti the other side of the unassuming entrance door should be enough to spur you on. Service is impeccable, authoritative and attentive, but Bossetti is happy to let customers just browse if that's what they want. He will also give private appointments out of working hours. In addition to the visionary vestments, there is plenty to adorn the home as well, including voluptuous fur throws and suede tassel pillows, oriental-style dining ceramics, and luxury bath and beauty ranges.

Because of the special relationship Concrete enjoys with its catwalk designer stars, it can customize designs to order – pending discussion, of course, on fabric, colour, size and so on. Naturallly this service isn't cheap, but remember we are talking 'major fashion moment' here. Concrete also stock the elusive one-off pieces you see in the shows and magazines but won't find in regular outlets because they're considered to be 'way too out there'. Unfortunately size-10s are the only ones able to take advantage of this service, but the pleasure of knowing your wardrobe contains the actual outfit Kate wore in Vogue last month might just do it for you.

COURTYARD

Courtyard
5–6 Angelgate
Guildford
Surrey
GU1 4AN
01483 452 825
Open: Mon–Sat 9.30–5.30

Angelgate in Guildford is a characterful cobbled side street, away from the homogenized main shopping precinct, and home to several independent womenswear outlets. Of these, Courtyard is the most progressive and also the busiest.

Owner Julia Jaconelli opened Courtyard seven years ago, but it's only now that she feels that the store is really how she wants it to be. She previously ran an outlet in Cheam (Bounce for Sportswear), but on moving to Guildford immediately spotted the gap in the market for designerwear. Initially, she kept the name Bounce and stocked safer labels such as Mulberry and Paul Costelloe, aiming for a more mature clientele. Since then, however, she has renamed the store and now opts for fresher British names with a more contemporary image.

Courtyard has an exclusive club-like feel. The quaint cottage-style exterior of white wood is counterbalanced by a very modern plate-glass window, displaying a variety of looks from the likes of Paul Smith and Megan Park. The interior is a mélange of pale greys and fawns, creating a sense of space in spite of the low ceilings. Elaborate glass-and-iron sculptures and two tall candelabra framing a central mirror create an almost baroque elegance. There are three good-sized fitting rooms.

The shop is divided into two main sections: funky/casual and smart/dressy. Jaconelli is aware that quality is of prime importance to her customers, whether they're looking for a pair of jeans or a graceful summer dress. Jaconelli's right-hand woman and manager is Suzie Smith, and her staff are notably approachable, adaptable and reassuringly fashion-conscious, their varying ages and images mirroring the diversity of the clientele. There is no hard-sell here, and the ambience is relaxed. Service is of a uniformly high standard but clearly focused on the core clientele of Surrey 'women who lunch'. Typically, customers are aged between twenty and forty-five and include quite a few mothers with young children, as the provision of toys testifies. One-on-one appointments are available, with very flexible hours offered.

The store continues to introduce and support up-and-coming fashion names. Jaconelli clearly wants to steer clear of the 'tried and tested', making Courtyard a forward-thinking boutique that stands head and shoulders above its neighbouring rivals.

THE CROSS

The Cross
141 Portland Road
London
W11 4LR
020 7727 6760
Open: Mon – Sat 10.30 – 6

Deep in the heart of Ladbroke Grove, amongst the brightly painted houses and bijou stores and restaurants, resides The Cross. Richly endowed with a plethora of clothes, gifts, homewares, toiletries and accessories, this all-white boutique offers a bewilderingly wide choice of products at a full range of prices points. This is a store that's very much an extension of the identities of owners Sarah Keen and Sam Robinson, and their strict policy is to buy what they like and not what fashion dictates. The result is an alluring pot-pourri of good and lovely things.

Despite the store's slightly reserved atmosphere, staff are friendly and the chilled Latin beats relaxing. Upstairs houses gifts, nightwear, childrenswear and beauty, as well as some clothing ranges such as denims. Downstairs, though, is the real fashion floor, with designs luxuriously displayed in every last bit of space. There's everything here that a West End girl could desire – from feminine daywear to classy evening separates and sexy nightwear. Sumptuous shoes by Rodolphe Menudier and Ann-Louise Roswald, together with a good selection of bags and jewellery, are available to complete a head-to-toe transformation.

There are three fitting rooms, two of which are secluded but doorless alcoves, decorated with kitsch sparkling lips and hearts and pink-and-black fluffy rugs. Feminine, flouncy and fairly fabulous, this store is pure fashion candy, leaving you hungry for more.

DIVERSE

Diverse
294 Upper Street,
London
N1 2TU
020 7359 8877
Open: Mon – Sat 10.30 – 6.30
Sun 12.30 – 5.30

Islington's vibrant Upper Street is home to the stylish Diverse, with dedicated womenswear and menswear branches. Diverse has come a long way from its beginnings in 1986. Originally run by owner Gabrielle Parker as an outlet for her printed textiles and T-shirt designs, it soon transformed into fashion central, especially after Parker was joined by daughter Saskia – also a Central Saint Martin's graduate. Today this North London must-have HQ is home to all the big names – Chloé, Matthew Williamson, Clements Ribeiro and Philosophy – as well as an evolving stable of some of the UK's most exciting young labels, including House of Jazz, Markus Lupfer, i.e.Uniform and Fake London. Even accessories and jewellery have been carefully selected to give as much variety as possible, encompassing pieces by the likes of Lara Bohinc, Ben Orr and Jade Jagger.

The store is arranged on two levels. Downstairs is funky and frenetic, while upstairs is decidedly chilled, housing both new collections and homeware. Both floors are spacious with pink walls, seagrass matting and central glass island cash desks. Clothes hang from rails around the edge of each room, while accessories turn up in unexpected areas, making the kind of ingenious styling suggestions that flick the switch on an outfit from just plain to plain interesting.

New design is sourced from all over the world, with Italy, France, New York, London, the Far East and Scandinavia making a particularly strong showing. Every country, it seems, has something to offer this mother-and-daughter combo. Saskia photographs the new collections and produces look-books, enabling the nine sales staff to know just what items are coming in for next season and how to style them. Customers are welcome to use these books as inspiration, too.

The key to this shop is its approach to service, which, says Parker, is about liking people and wanting to communicate with them. 'We want to make it easy for everybody to appreciate good design by putting it on a plate for them. Everything is cherry-picked, including our staff, whom the customers often ask for by name.' If you chose your time well – let's say Monday morning rather than Saturday afternoon – you can have as much one-to-one service as you want. Of course, if you walk away with a bit of kit in a carrier that's even better, but there's no pressure to purchase. This is, after all, a fashion haven where to be individual is to be 'diverse'.

DULWICH TRADER

The Dulwich Trader
9 Croxted Road
London
SE21 8SZ
020 8761 3457

Tomlinson's
89 Dulwich Village
London
SE21 7BJ
020 8299 1260

Ed
41 Northcross Road
London
SE22 9ET
020 8299 6938

Open: Mon – Sat 9.30 – 6
Sun 11 – 5

When it comes to independent retailing in the well-to-do London suburb of Dulwich, the Tomlinsons have the market sewn up. The Dulwich Trader, Tomlinson's and Ed are three very contrasting stores located in West, North and East Dulwich respectively. Each store has its own vivid personality, but all three provide a complete shopping experience, stocking all kinds of desirables from furniture to stationery, as well as an ever-growing range of branded designer clothing and accessories. The connecting factor that links this disparate array is that, thanks to ingenious buying, every product has a truly special, hand-picked quality.

The Dulwich Trader is the oldest and largest store of the group, founded in 1989 and situated on a shopping parade in affluent West Dulwich.

Penny Tomlinson, a former publishing executive, began the business on a whim. Pretty quickly the shop escalated beyond her control, and her husband, Chris, had to be taken on board to handle the business side of things. Tomlinson's buying ethos is constantly evolving. 'At first we were looking for quality, affordable clothing, now we are going the other way, with more expensive brands that are often impulse buys, such as Jennifer Dagworthy, Artwork and Day. People want exclusivity.'

The level of personal service is quite spectacular, and styling advice is honest and caring. Much of the success of the Dulwich Trader is due to the hands-on management of Chris Roberts, but it is obvious that all the staff genuinely love what they do and want to get involved. The owners have devised a unique customer evening, in which just three or four clients are served by the same number of staff. This makes for an intimate shopping experience, allowing women who are usually afraid to step out of the fitting rooms to flaunt what they wear with confidence.

Tomlinson's, the second branch, opened in 1993 and is commonly referred to as 'the village shop'. Carrying a selected range of brands from The Dulwich Trader, this ultra-feminine boutique focuses more on shoes and accessories. In complete contrast, Ed is where you'll find the funk. Founded in 1999 and located in up-and-coming East Dulwich, it has already achieved great critical acclaim as a fun, hip store that doesn't take itself too seriously.

EGO

LABELS
Armani Jeans
Cavalli
Ghost
James Lakeland
Juicy Couture
Kenzo
Patrick Mendes
Phillipe Adec
Pringle
Save the Queen
Shirin Guild
Zucchero

ACCESSORIES
Luis Estere
Missoni

SIZES
8 – 18

RETURNS POLICY
Exchange or credit note
within 14 days

Ego
102 – 104 Watling Street
Radlett
Hertfordshire
WD7 7AB
01923 852 843
Open: Mon – Fri 9.30 – 6
Sat 9 – 6

The leafy, affluent commuter town of Radlett is home to Ego, an independent, classy store offering a comprehensive range of designer clothes for men and women. When they bought the Radlett shop some twenty years ago, Melvyn and Judy Sims were already running a menswear shop in Tunbridge Wells. They went on to open outlets in St. John's Wood and Golders Green. Since then, they have gradually pared the business down to enable them to focus on this, their flagship store. The Sims work together, both in terms of buying and staff management.

The interior of Ego is classic and unfussy, and there are clear parallels with high-street names such as Next. Unthreatening muzak sets the relaxed tone of the store, and staff are more than attentive, reflecting the fact that this is a friendly, family-run business.

There is a real feeling of community here, and service is of a very high standard. The customer through-flow at Ego is high, so the staff – of whom at least four are on duty at at any one time – and the five fitting rooms are kept very busy.

The Sims are happy to order out-of-stock items for customers, and, refreshingly, there is a free alteration service for non-sale goods. Classic tailoring dominates the menswear ranges, while womenswear is more casual and evening oriented. Ego's selling point, however, is the unquestionable quality of customer service.

ENVY

Envy
51 High Street
Cobham
Surrey
KT11 3DP
01932 863 484
Open: Mon – Sat 9 – 5.30

Envy illustrates everything *Fashion UK* is about: quality designer clothing sold with exceptional service and without pretension – in our opinion the fundamental ingredients for every good womenswear store. For this relative newcomer to the competitive world of retail (the store opened in 2000), prospects certainly look bright.

Located in a 200-year-old listed cottage that was previously home to another high-class boutique, Envy successfully bridges old and new, classic and funky. Like many of the entrepreneurs featured in this book, owner and buyer Gerry Lovick had no previous fashion experience, but through sheer passion for good design and effervescence managed to extend the shop's appeal to younger, trendier shoppers while maintaining the interest of the existing, more mature clientele. Fresh designer names such as Joseph, Donna Karen and Hugo Boss have here joined timeless, classic brands such as Escada, Joyce Riding and Jean Muir to good effect.

Service is attentive, personal and – last but not least – honest. The two luxurious fitting rooms in a secluded area at the back of the boutique have an

almost consulting-room feel to them. Alterations are available, and regular calls are made to clients to invite them to view pre-selected ranges. Lovick is also a very active charity worker and often puts on large-scale fashion shows to raise money.

Lovick's warm, friendly personality radiates throughout the store. 'I treat all my potential customers with a genuine respect', she says, 'whether they're wearing Gucci or Wellington boots or spending £50 or £200!' Her buying decisions are usually based on instinct, which, she says, hasn't led her astray yet, and her choice of clothes is simple, elegant and feminine. There are very few accessories, but a select choice of elaborate handbags designed by Maria di Ripabianca will put the finishing touches to what is sure to be an enviable look.

EVA

Eva
12 High Street
Ipswich
Suffolk
IP1 3JX
01473 236 650
Open: Mon – Sat 9.30 – 5

At first glance, Eva's sparse reception area might seem intimidating. An elaborate Persian carpet, however, exudes the promise of exotica, and as you climb the stairs, three abstract pictures brighten the gallery-like interior and beckon you higher. There are four sections in this spacious store, with the stretch between making a perfect catwalk for the seasonal fashion shows that take place here.

Owner Jana Khayat purchased Eva in 1999, taking a year to give the store a complete refurbishment. Khayat – a former fashion buyer at London's Fortnum & Mason – is clearly no stranger to the industry and knows how to listen to her customers. Clients of the shop's prevous incarnation had complained about its strictly 8–12 sizing policies, so now Eva stocks a selection of designers able to offer more realistically proportioned clothes as well as those who deliver larger size ranges. Eva's policy is, Khayat says, 'to live and learn' – which in practice means following the needs of customers rather than the dictates of fashion.

'Quality, Luxury and Accessibility' is the mantra for those who serve at Eva. Staff are smart and well-dressed but not overly formal, helping to create the store's relaxed and open atmosphere. 'We don't pounce, and we don't follow people', says the management. Private appointments are always on offer, and staff will keep the shop open after hours if need be. Everyone who comes to Eva – from local secretaries to titled ladies – are given the same comprehensive and friendly service.

Khayat is clearly proud of her store's personal touch. The old computerized system, for example, has been abandoned in favour of handwritten receipts and colour-coded files. Old-fashioned as such changes may appear, they nevertheless encourage better staff-customer relations by placing the emphasis on the person rather than the inputting of information.

The fashion shows – organized to raise money for charity and to promote new stock – are put carefully together, combining professional models with excellent food and wine. The shows have been such a success that Eva is now exploring more customer-oriented activities, such as fun shopping days and evenings that will include advice from well-known London stylists.

LABELS
John Smedley
Joseph
Matthew Williamson
Mr and Mrs MacLeod
Nicole Farhi
Paul Smith
Phillipe Adec
Pringle
Quentin and Chadwick
Strenesse
Voyage Passion

ACCESSORIES
Anya Hindmarch
Camper
Robert Cleregie
Kellin

SIZES
8 – 16

RETURNS POLICY
Exchange within
28 days

Fluidity
43 Bell Street
Henley-on-Thames
Oxfordshire
RG9 2BA
01491 412 323
Open: Mon – Sat 9.30 – 5.50

The beautiful riverside town of Henley is home to Fluidity – a haven of minimalist elegance. Simplicity is clearly the unifying concept here. The sparse window display, featuring perhaps just a single item – a bag or a shoe – allows passers-by to see right into the store.

The interiors are spacious, modern and fresh, with wooden panelling, delicate drop lighting and turquoise and sky-blue fixtures. The ambience is reassuringly tranquil. Instead of music, there's the murmur of running water from ceramic water features sited close to the store entrance. Owner Suzie Harvey-Clarke explains that she is 'obsessed with not breaking the concentration of the shopper. I love music, but it's a powerful medium and the wrong choice can throw some people off and create the wrong mood.'

Her choice of clothes show a similar restraint. When buying, Harvey-Clarke strictly avoids transitory fashion fads; her focus is on the slower, more measured evolution of fashion design. Tasteful merchandizing emphasizes the sleek, well-cut clothing range, which features a core staple of black, broken by slashes of bold colour. The aim is to inspire and excite customers by providing an individual choice of core pieces that can form the basis of an all-embracing, definitive wardrobe.

Fluidity clearly cherishes its loyal clientele. Service is notably personal, with customers frequently welcomed by their first names. The core client base is aged mostly between thirty and fifty-five, a group for whom the one-on-one service and astute styling advice given by Harvey-Clarke and her team are especially important attractions. Fluidity's recent expansion into menswear with F2 (at 8 Duke Street) has also proved thoroughly successful, and Harvey-Clarke still toys with the idea of opening a store aimed directly at younger women.

FOOTLIGHTS

LABELS

Betsey Johnson
DKNY
Dolce & Gabbana
Jeans
Frankie B
Kenzo
120% Linen
Rachel Robart
Versace
Votre Nom

ACCESSORIES

Dolce & Gabbana
Joomi Joolz

SIZES

8 – 16

RETURNS POLICY

Credit note on goods
returned within 28 days

Footlights
21 Oakdene Parade
Cobham
Surrey
KT11 2LR
01932 860 190
Open: Mon – Sat 9.30 – 5.30

Commuter-belt Cobham in Surrey is home to a number of good independent fashion retailers. Of these, Footlights has cornered the high-fashion market, plying labels such as Dolce & Gabbana, Versace and DKNY. The store's black-and-gold exterior houses a simple but well-heeled boutique, its air of luxury drawing a label-motivated fashion crowd.

The shop began twenty-one years ago. Proprietor Belinda Harris inherited the business from her mother and still does much of the buying with her sister Erica. There have been several shops in Knightsbridge, Kingston and Surbiton, but the business has finally settled in Surrey, which is where its strongest customer base resides. Originally a dance- and casualwear boutique (hence the name), Footlights shifted its focus to fashion in the mid-1990s, retailing classic, high-status brands. The store caters to women who demand exclusivity, so Harris is always careful to buy in just one or two of each design.

Customers only rarely make appointments, but a personal service is always given to those who demand it. That said, staff are also happy to let browsers browse. Sales staff are professional and warm and give great service; they often make personal calls to keep the clientele up-to-date on the latest must-haves. Tea and coffee is provided, and the shop is pram-friendly. There are two fitting rooms constructed from luxury drapes, but there is less privacy if both cubicles are in use.

Harris is a woman who knows what she and her clientele want, and customers of every age trust her to get it for them – whether it's newsworthy fashions or up-to-the-minute classics, eye-catching daywear or glamorous eveningwear. There is a strong feeling of community in the shop. This is the place where regulars who enjoy the thrill of fashion-industry gossip and local news, and the strong feminine energy provided by Harris herself go to get 'buzzed up' and 'kitted out'.

THE GLASSHOUSE

The Glasshouse
15 East Street
Brighton
East Sussex
BN1 1HP
01273 326 141
www.the-glasshouse.co.uk
Open: Mon – Sat 9.30 – 6
Sun 11 – 4

Additional branches in Guildford,
Richmond and Windsor

With its wide, fast-changing range of independents, bustling seaside Brighton is a retail paradise for a wide range of shoppers – both locals and tourists alike. The Glasshouse, owned and run by Helen Gregory and Janice Culshaw, stands serene in the midst of this frenetic environment, its soft-grey exterior and delicate white lettering promising a quiet haven for those unconcerned by current trends and fashion fads. The company slogan, promising a retail destination for 'real women', sums up the Glasshouse approach to sizing and design.

This Brighton store is the latest branch to open in a chain of four. In each, a uniform, grey-on white interior is the backdrop to a large, abstract silk painting by Ann Trewartha reflecting the local area and its inhabitants. In Brighton, the painted pebbles, sand and sea underline the store's free-flowing and relaxed attitude to clothes – functional yet exotic designs for women of all shapes and sizes. The average customer at Glasshouse is size 16, and Gregory and Culshaw design and buy with this in mind.

Stock is bought in from a selection of mainly European designers. The labels are exclusive to The Glasshouse in the UK; if a brand becomes too widely available, it is replaced with something new to preserve the stock's individuality. Each season Gregory and Culshaw buy first, and then fill in the gaps with their own, high-quality range, which is designed by Gregory and manufactured all over the world. The Glasshouse is also able to make garments to order, its versatility made possible by long-standing relationships with manufacturers.

Designs are merchandized in contrasting colours and alongside displays of stunning, handmade pieces of jewellery. Staff, led by manager Sasha Miller Hudson, are lively and talkative and offer friendly, helpful service. Should you find yourself planning a first-time visit, try going on a Saturday, when the store often throws an impromptu party of wine and nibbles.

LABELS
Bita Kai Rand
Cut Loose
Esmerelda
Flax
Frequence
Glasshouse
Hebbeding

ACCESSORIES
Cherabe
Phillippe Aubibeat
Pilgrim
Pold

SIZES
8 – 18 (up to 26 in
free-size garments)

RETURNS POLICY
No refunds on
non-faulty goods;
exchange or credit
note within 7 days

The Glass house

Gotham Angels
23 Islington Green
London
N1 8DU
020 7359 8090
www.gotham-angels.com
Open: Mon – Fri 10.30 – 7
Sat 10 – 6
Sun 12 – 6

GOTHAM ANGELS

When the well-heeled shoppers of London's fashionable N1 want to feel the funk, they gravitate to the heavenly hangout that is Gotham Angels. There they can team beautifully made garments with sparklers from the house jewellery range (Gotham Rock) or, if they are feeling altruistic, kit their daughters out in the children's range (Gotham Devils).

Owners and founders Sara Maragh and Kate Keene met while independently designing for some of the biggest UK names, having been snapped up on graduating from Central Saint Martin's and the Royal College respectively. They discovered they shared a desire to manufacture their own designs whose common accent was on individuality and an appeal to spirited women of all ages. They've stayed true to their original desire to create clothes that are fashion-led but not about trends, and they don't sell anything they wouldn't wear themselves.

The advent of the children's range reflects their changing lives. On becoming mothers, both saw a gap in the market and plugged it with clothes that are pretty but not overly girly. Miniature punky T-shirts are practically framable but perfect all the same for sticky little hands. And true to their roots, Maragh and Keene also put in the hours sourcing lines from the young talent emerging from the colleges, allowing them to rub hangers with more established names.

The shops themselves reflect the design ethos. Both the Islington and Crouch End branches cocoon clients in a warm cloud, lit with fairy lights and studded with bejewelled cacti. The ambience is eclectic and on the right side of kitsch. The music policy is chic but mature – funk, blues, Eighties classics. The staff – often students – are creative and fashion-literate, picked as much for their personalities as the cut of their jibs. Every Friday two of them dress the window, crafting a modern mural of womenswear must-haves to inspire and fascinate passers-by.

The store's clientele cover all ages, but the core are aged twenty to thirty-five. The stance is very pro-customer, and the owners – aware that tastes alter with age – make sure that buying reflects the changing needs of their clients. There's something for everyone here – even for celebrities, who can drop in safe in the knowledge that there will be no fuss. Service is personal; there's a customer database, and calls are made when the right item comes in. New collections are shown at customer evenings, with wine and discounts of course!

GUILIO

LABELS
Armani
Burberry
Custo
Earl Jeans
Etro
Evisu
Fake London
Gucci
Hugo Boss
Paul Smith
Prada
Prada Sport

ACCESSORIES
Burberry
Christian Dior
Evisu
Gucci
Prada
Prada Sport

SIZES
6 – 14

RETURNS POLICY
Exchange or credit
note within 14 days

Guilio
5 – 7 Sussex Street
Cambridge
Cambridgeshire
CB1 1PA
01223 316 166
Open: Mon – Fri 9 – 5.30
Sat 9 – 6

Guilio (Menswear)
24 – 32 King Street
Cambridge
CB1 1LN
01223 316 180
Open: Mon – Fri 9 – 5.30
Sat 9 – 6

The architecturally beautiful city of Cambridge is home to the independent retailer Guilio. Since the first branch opened some twenty-two years ago, Guilio has built an enviable reputation as one of the city's leading stores, and this has been confirmed by the recent launch of its excellent womenswear branch.

The new store is housed in a magnificent period building with dramatic exterior pillars and ultra-modern, concave tinted windows. The minimalist interior is a mixture of harsh greys but is cleverly warmed by the use of underlit furnishings, designed by the owner, Guilio Cinque. Garments are displayed separately, almost as if they were works of art. After all, Cinque notes, 'We don't sell the fashion equivalent of baked beans.' Clearly a feeling for space comes high on the agenda here. The operations manager, Sian Wicklow, cites her pet retail hate as 'being trapped in a store with so many clothes crammed in that you can't see

anything'. It's not just a question of aesthetics, though; it's also a matter of access: 'Mums with buggies need to get around and sometimes it's nice to be able to get away from the sales assistants!' The fitting rooms (of which there are four in all) are likewise exceptionally large.

The unashamedly exclusive feel and appearance of Guilio may be discouraging to some, and the young model-like staff could also be seen as intimidating. Venture in, though, and you'll find that the assistants are friendly and informative, and their styling abilities strong. Personal shopping could be said to be the norm here, rather than the exception, though appointments are available. An alteration service is available to customers for a small fee.

The customer base at Guilio is surprisingly diverse, and ages range from around twenty-five to fifty. The store is acutely aware that their Cambridge location is to some extent limiting, in that their customers tend not to be quite so adventurous as their London counterparts. Nevertheless, both Guilio stores are highly impressive ventures with unifying themes of exclusivity and über-stylishness.

HERO

LABELS
Armani Collezioni
Chine
Ghost
Joseph
Nicole Farhi
Philosophy
Sherrin Guild

ACCESSORIES
Anya Hindmarch
Blue Gem
Dybergkern
Emma Hope
Erva

SIZES
8–16

RETURNS POLICY
Refund for goods
returned within one
week, with receipt;
credit note for
goods returned
after one week.

Hero
3 Green Street
Cambridge
Cambridgeshire
CB2 3JU
01223 328 740
Open: Mon – Sat 9.30 – 5.30

In one of Cambridge's numerous quaint passageways is the stalwart independent Hero, a wonderfully welcoming boutique devoted to everything from classic womenswear to 'boho' style and just about everything between. Its mint-green Georgian frontage is refreshingly unpretentious. Inside, the stylized sloping walls – designed by Ted Walters – consist of various white and deep-blue contours.

Despite its modest size, the shop stocks an impressive range of designers, but somehow manages to feel uncluttered. On the ground floor is daywear and casualwear, while eveningwear is on the first floor, where an antique turquoise chandelier adds a fairy-tale touch to the proceedings. Each floor has two large fitting rooms, and upstairs is a comfortable seating area, perfect for those accompanying would-be Cinderellas.

Owner and buyer Lesley de la Mare began her working career in real estate and ventured into fashion only after raising a family. 'No one can ever prepare you for everything when it comes to independent retailing. It's a lot of hard work, and no amount of research or analysis can prevent you from making errors. Fashion is illogical, and you have to take risks when buying. For a small store with a modest expenditure things can be difficult dealing with big, established names.' A decade on, de la Mare's calm exterior shows a woman well versed in fashion industry goings-on, someone who won't be pushed into ordering above her means. Nevertheless, she still buys in the same way she did when she was just a beginner – using gut instinct. Sourcing new labels is an important pursuit for this retailer, adding an element of surprise to the impressive collection of big names already selling in the shop.

The welcoming staff are diverse stylewise, but their shared flair for fashion allows for a comprehensive styling service. Their talents can be employed out of hours, too. New incoming collections will be sorted through for size and taste and delivered directly to the door. Other services include an overhaul of customers' entire wardrobe.

Lesley de la Mare has always been aware of how important price and quality is to her customers, and strives for the best in both categories. Regular shoppers are often creative types, but the age range is broad. The store is fast becoming one of the town's main attractions, drawing in fashion tourists from the surrounding counties and beyond.

INDIGO

LABELS
Adolfo Dominguez
Annette Gortz
Anne Storey
B.I. Blues
Caractère
Cerutti 1881
James Lakeland
Lamberto Losani
Strenesse Blue
Tombilini
Whistles

ACCESSORIES
Orla Kiely

SIZES
8 – 16

RETURNS POLICY
Exchange within
14 days

Indigo
1 – 2 Baffins Lane
Chichester
West Sussex
PO19 1UA
01243 789 099
Open: Mon – Sat 9.30 – 5.30

Situated just off Chichester's smart pedestrianized high street is Indigo – a small, bright, independent boutique stocking a variety of fresh and feminine clothing. Owner Heidi De Fries – a graduate from the London College of Fashion – has a very progressive attitude to fashion and aims her collections very much at the 'ageless woman of the 21st century'. After graduating, De Fries developed her buying and manufacturing skills mainly overseas, but eventually took the plunge and set up her own business in the UK. In the intervening four or so years Indigo has simply gone from strength to strength.

The modern yellow-and-purple exterior is eye-catching, and the creative, alluring window displays are instantly inviting. Interiors are 'contemporary-classic'; wooden floors and white walls set the scene for delicately designed iron and glass fittings. Merchandize is immaculately colour-coordinated, and

simplicity not gimmickry seem to be the watchwords here. Indigo offers an uncomplicated shopping experience for women spanning three generations, reflected in the discerning selection of tasteful yet timeless fashion.

Stock covers the full spectrum of casualwear, smart daywear and simple evening pieces. When sourcing merchandize, De Fries is particularly attracted to the more obscure venues. She is always keen, she says, to seek out genuinely new and innovative pieces that will offset the ranges of her core brands. She buys primarily in Paris, London and Milan, utilizing her fashion training to select the finest-quality fabrics.

There is a noticeably relaxed ambience. Approachable staff dressed from head to toe in Indigo merchandize glide serenely around the store attending to customers. Styling advice is readily offered, and De Fries herself often takes appointments outside opening hours. It's not unusual for pieces to be ordered in larger sizes, with customers under no obligation to purchase. All the clothes here are barcoded and relate to a complex database of who buys what garments and in which size. This enables Indigo to successfully monitor – and respond to – the needs of their loyal clientele.

JEANNE PETITT

Jeanne Petitt
3 Bridge Street
Hungerford
Berkshire
RG17 OEH
01488 682 472
Open: Mon – Sat 9.30 – 5

The village of Hungerford, with its winding canal and surrounding Berkshire countryside, is an idyllic place. A small bridge leading down to the town centre is home to a handful of independent retailers, primarily featuring antiques dealers and hunting shops, but also a French-style boutique, with a simple black front and languid gold italic sign. This is Jeanne Petitt.

The magnolia interior, with its sea-grass floor, has a charmingly rural feel. Hand-painted murals adorn the walls, while wooden baker's racks are used to display accessories. The shop is divided into three distinct sections – daywear, eveningwear and accessories – plus a conservatory that accommodates a range of lingerie and swimwear (available all year). There is a large private dressing-room, although individual cubicles are a little small. A comfy sofa and beautiful large garden makes shopping with tired partners or small children a pleasure, and toys and biscuits are liberally proffered. The atmosphere here is relaxed; the staff are charming.

The owner, Sarah Petitt, inherited the shop from her mother, but had previously never envisaged running her own fashion store. She took to it, however, with some aplomb. Over time, she has gradually expanded and updated many of the labels stocked, and nowadays the focus is on elegant simple pieces that nevertheless have something sexy or exciting about them – as Petitt notes of the store's overall image, 'classic but never dull'. Petitt is available for personal appointments, and places a high value on building and maintaining close relations with her customers.

JOY

Joy
432 Coldharbour Lane
Brixton
London SW9 8LG
020 7787 9616
Open: Mon – Sat 10 – 7.30
Sun 1 – 7

393 King Street
Chiswick
London W6 9NJ
020 8741 8183
Open: Mon – Sat 10 – 7.30
Sun 1 – 7

9 Nelson Road
Greenwich
SE10 9JB
020 8293 7979
Open: Mon – Sat 10 – 7.30
Sun 1 – 7.30

Joy, the fashion/lifestyle emporium, has been a resounding critical and commercial success since it opened in Brixton in 1999. Housing everything from eclectic clothing and accessory designs for men and women, to bizarre gift paraphernalia, this contemporary bazaar delivers the maximum amount of merchandise per square inch. For a growing number of urban creatives its their favourite shop.

A visit to this vast 2500ft^2 style depot, through the custom-made chunky cast-iron rusting door frame, reveals a variety of options. Should you investigate the mountain of amusing knick-knacks as you navigate the organised chaos in front of you? Peruse the rails of affordable, edgy, women's fashion? Or steer your gaze skywards and admire the extraordinary ceiling display – a patchwork of authentic 1930's design, especially acquired for the store and patched up unashamedly with newly crafted copper pieces? If in doubt, head for the gigantic mirror on the far left of the store etched with the words 'Goddess Of Glamour' and simply enjoy your own marvellousness while you hang out with a friendly sales person.

Joy is the creation of owner and former fashion designer Maureen O'Brien, and has been celebrated in print as a '21st-century Biba'. Her 'pile it up and encourage shoppers to root around for it' approach, is instinctive, yet considered. 'Clothes are no fun if they are just handed over – women enjoy feeling they have found something unique', says O'Brien. The disordered shop floor however is in contrast to the orderly backroom where a database of around 3000 shoppers is held.

Core customers tend to be aged twenty to forty, well read, media types and with that in mind sales assistants picked for their style savvy and retail backgrounds can offer a personal shopping experience with style and fashion advice as a staple.

The USP of Joy is its constantly changing stock. One garment in each size range ensures individuality and O'Brien buys all year round – sourcing unknowns as well as established brands. Importantly, with twenty-five years in fashion design for names like Mexx and Benetton, the owner of Joy can spot and eliminate a badly made garment in her sleep.

Expanding quickly, new branches of Joy are planned for Clapham and Soho.

KOKON TO ZAI

Kokon to Zai
57 Greek Street
London
W1D 3DX
020 7434 1316
Open: Mon – Sat 11 – 7.30
Sun 12 – 5

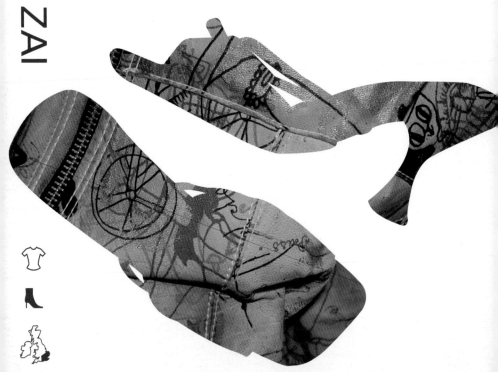

Located in the hubbub of London's trendy Soho, eccentric retail outlet Kokon to Zai, with its arresting window displays mixing artistry and erotica, may intimidate the faint-hearted. But for those who seek a boutique experience that's right on the cutting-edge of contemporary culture, this shop, with its on-site DJs, crucifixes, unicorns and skeletons, will hit the spot. Half the premises is a record store, allowing visiting Soho bohos to combine a unique fashion fix with a leisured trawl through vinyl rarities.

Kokon to Zai is owned by music-man-cum-manager Sasha B and designer-cum-art director Marjan Pejoski, who recently started his own label (exclusively available in the store for its first season). The shop first opened in London in 1996, and a second, larger branch followed in Paris in 2000.

Homing in on non-commercial, original designers, many of whom are recent fashion graduates, and selecting quirkier pieces by more established designers, the store showcases undiscovered looks and one-offs, fusing music, fashion and art in a perfect marriage of unconventional taste. Stock is constantly changing and often transcends retail trends. The store has an exhibition space, displaying fine art, fashion and video installations – in fact anything art-based that is truly new and inspiring.

Kokon to Zai aims to inspire rather than prescribe – the only imperative here is to be experimental. The range of jewellery and accessories is surprisingly broad but just as unsurprisingly avant-garde – Weekend Pussy's leather and human hair accessories may not be everyone's cup of tea but are certainly good conversation starters. Shoes are to-die-for. Vinti Andrews practically sculpts boots in draped and deconstructed fabrics and leathers, while the collection from Paul Andrews consisted of two-tone woven-denim designs. Staff are warm, welcoming and helpful.

The big challenge for customers, though, is the changing room, which takes the form of a circular curtain tucked away in a corner. The music types may give the place a more relaxed atmosphere than you might have expected, but some people may feel less than comfortable stripping off close to what feels like a dance floor. Kokon to Zai is a love-or-hate thing. Before you make up your mind, though, try it out for yourself. If it's tech house, progressive, break beat, hard house or electro beat that fits your groove, then the perfect soundtrack to a perfect afternoon's shopping may well await you.

MALAPA

Malapa
41 Clerkenwell Road
London
EC1M 5RS
020 7490 5229
Open: Mon – Fri 11 – 7

Malapa is a solitary clothes boutique on the busy Clerkenwell Road specializing in end-of-the-range designer garments and samples. Located at the heart of the new-media triangle (Clerkenwell, Shoreditch, Hoxton), the store attracts both fashion types and casual passers-by.

Owner Sharon Reid first opened the store in 1997, aiming 'to sell the best of new designers, especially the unconventional and the forward-thinking'. Inconsistent profits by the end of 2000, however, forced Reid to reassess her project. 'We always did well in sales… so I decided to test the water with a two-day sample sale. We profiled designers such as Dai Rees and Tristen Webber and took more in two days than in the entire month before! The only way forward was to continue as a sales outlet.' Knockdown prices, however, don't mean a drop in quality. As Reid points out: 'We sell cutting-edge labels, keeping the same high standards we had before.' Flushed with her new-found fiscal consistency, Reid has also extended her for-hire range of vintage one-offs, including Fifties cocktail dresses and slinky Seventies halternecks. There is a 'look-book' to aid selection, and items cost between £5 and £70 to loan.

Decor is simple but attractive. Inside, two silver rails running the length of the store, are packed with cutting-edge, colourful designs – some by recognized names, others by the less well-known. All of the clothing, however, has some special or interesting feature – an intricate cut or unusual fabric – and there's an innovative and intelligent choice of bags, belts and jewellery to match. Designs are purchased on a sale-or-return basis, and with new consignments delivered every week, it's well worth dropping in here on a regular basis.

Reid has an extensive mailing list but doesn't like to bombard customers with literature. She prefers a more personal touch, often developing close bonds with regulars. Service is unaffected and passionate, and Reid's love of what she's doing radiates throughout the store. 'I am emotionally attached to the business of retailing', she declares. Enjoying good relations with her regular designers, Reid can often get larger sizes made up especially, and has access to excellent tailoring and dry-cleaning services.

MATCHES

Matches
13 Hill Street
Richmond
Surrey
TW9 1FX
020 8332 9733
Open: Mon – Sat 10 – 6
Sun 12 – 6

60 – 64 Ledbury Road
London
W11 2AJ
020 7221 0255
Open: Mon – Sat 10 – 6
Sun 12 – 6

Matches provide a truly luxuriant shopping experience at the heart of some of London's most affluent residential enclaves. Owners Tom and Ruth Chapman opened the original Matches store in Wimbledon in 1984, gradually expanding the business to encompass eight stores throughout London, although five remain Wimbledon-based. Refreshingly in an age of chainstore homogeneity, each outlet has a distinct personality and offers a selection of some thirty-plus designers stocked exclusively to each area.

The Richmond store is housed in a beautiful old courthouse on the edge of the high street. Inside, the decor is elegantly understated, the contemporary mood enhanced by the use of original artworks provided by the Notting Hill gallery, Apart. A recent refurbishment has seen the inclusion of an 'airport-style lounge' area, underlining the Matches ethos of a relaxed and leisurely shopping experience. There is also a cappuccino bar to sustain weary shopping partners as well as a designated child-friendly play area.

With the womenswear collections situated on the ground floor and menwear in the basement, the store is very conducive to shopping with a partner. While you are perusing, enjoy the sense of fun emanating from the charming sales staff.

The opening of the Matches new flagship store in Ledbury Road at the end of 2000 confirmed the store's status as a competitive and independent force in

fashion. This branch – the height of cool with its shiny black-and-white interior and tasselled shop fixtures – has to be the ultimate haven for fashion darlings seeking the latest must-have designer purchases. Exclusivity abounds. A private-appointments area, which also doubles as a bar bathed in ambient purple lighting – is just one of the retail extras that attracts much celebrity attention. Be prepared to brush shoulders with Jude Law and Sadie Frost in the acid-green perspex fitting rooms or jostle with Alanis Morisette at the sales.

Designers are merchandized separately, stocking comprehensive ranges of well-known brands such as Prada, Gucci and D&G. The company maxim 'pigeon holes are for pigeons' is reflected in the innovative buying policy of Bridget Cosgrave, former international womenswear buyer for Harvey Nics. 'Every garment has to make the best of the woman it is appealing to', she says. 'I never buy ugly or intellectual clothing for the sake of new trends.' Standards of service are, of course, high. Anything from brunch to a St. Tropez tan can be ordered on demand. Staff will even happily courier a selection of clothes in your size to try on in the comfort of your own home – ideal for a last-minute special occasion.

Unconventionally, smoking is allowed in-store. Matches gets the balance right – a dreamy list of contemporary designers in a welcoming and receptive environment. True retail therapy.

N. Shelley
75 – 79 High Street
Billericay
Essex
CM12 9AS
01277 621 000
Open: Mon – Sat 9 – 5.30

This impeccable womenswear shop is housed in a black-and-white grade II-listed cottage that has stood on Billericay's high street for more than four hundred years. Since 1928, N. Shelley has provided good quality casual clothing, suiting, lingerie, accessories, beachwear and occasion outfits to a mostly local clientele of all ages. The secret of the success of this century-spanning family-run business has been the service, calm, affable environment, and the priority given to customer needs over fashion dictates.

Proprietor Sarah Millet – the great-niece of the store's founder, Norah Shelley – took over the store eight years ago. Her experience of working as a buyer at the Burton Group's head office provided her with the knowledge to expand the designer range. She is always on the lookout for fresh labels and particularly favours Italian, Spanish, German and Dutch manufacturers. She is keen for her collection to be current, but is just as keen that it remains true to the essence of 'what real women want'. 'Being small', she adds, 'has advantages, too. With overnight door-to-door deliveries we don't have to buy large quantities…we can get repeat orders within 48 hours.'

Although only one of each style is ever displayed, by mid-season the store is densely stocked with offerings from more than sixty suppliers. This embarrassment of riches allows N. Shelley to cater for every age of woman, with a wide variety of looks and sizes. A particular plus is the outstanding range of trousers – 700, in fact, in almost every cut and colour. Even if you can't see what you want, staff are happy to call manufacturers to see if they can accommodate.

Exquisite fashion displays arranged by Millet's able assistant Abi Cashran (a graduate of the London College of Fashion) bring a refreshing energy to this classic establishment. The interior of beige, black, ivory and peach is luxurious but unfussy, and there's an upstairs lounge area where customers can relax and make their mind up about purchases. Staff are smart, helpful and dedicated, offering a genuinely personal experience, from styling to general advice. They often visit customers at home, and appointments after hours are no problem. Free alterations and luxury gift-wrapping are basic services at this store, which prides itself on offering honest prices for all rather than discounts for a few.

If your lust for shopping is still not sated after a visit to this store, then try out the separate N. Shelley accessories store just two doors down the street. There you'll find an irresistible range of perfect styling accoutrements, including bags, jewellery, hats, sunglasses and scarves by names such as Suzy Smith, Dior and Dyberg Kern.

Rellik
8 Golborne Road
London
W10 5NW
020 8962 0089
Open: Tues – Sat 10 – 6

LABELS
Affinity
Identity (Ozzie Clark,
Zandra Rhodes
Jean Muir)
Laissez Faire
Vivienne Westwood

SIZES
8 – 12

RETURNS POLICY
Refunds at manager's
discretion; item must
have ticket in place.

Rellik is a vintage treasure-trove, buried deep in the urban undergrowth of west London and overshadowed by the infamous Trellik Tower housing estate. The location may not be upmarket, but for some this may add to its appeal. 'It's an interesting part of town', says co-owner Steve Philip, 'giving customers the feeling that they might just discover something completely individual'. An entry bell adds to the off-the-beaten-track, exclusive feel. The store acts as an umbrella for its three designer-proprietors – Steve Philip, Claire Stansfield and Fiona Carenza – and the key to its success is its hybrid take on style. There are three labels. Identity by Philip offers customers the chance to relive or reinvent the past through an array of historic fashion pieces from the Twenties to the Nineties – clothing, jewellery, bags, shoes and hats – everything in impeccable condition. Laissez Faire (by Stansfield) and Affinity (by Carenza) largely consist of new looks customized from antique fabrics. Many of the pieces are one-offs or limited editions, so the air of exclusivity hangs thick.

As you might expect, the store is a visual feast. All manner of delectable and precious things await in an interior of exposed brickwork and concave glass tiles: a pair of Westwood platforms in lime croc skin, just like the ones that infamously toppled Naomi Campbell; a 1970 Ossie Clark shell-colour crêpe coat with frill neckline; or a newly minted piece from Stansfield and Carenza's on-site workshop. Faced with such gorgeous offerings, you can easily say goodbye to the outside world for an hour or two. Rellik is no stranger to the magazine write-up, but it doesn't actively court publicity and prefers the vibe you get from word-of-mouth. 'The people who come to see us are all looking for adventure', says Philip. It's certainly best not to come here with a fixed idea of what you want – just give your senses free rein and let your imagination soar. Staff are easy-going and happy to help, and there's a real feeling of everybody – even celebrities – just mucking in.

SEFTON

Sefton
271 Upper Street
London
N1 2UQ
020 7226 9822
Open: Mon – Wed 10 – 6.30
Thurs – Fri 10 – 7
Sat 10 – 6.30
Sun 12 – 5.30

22 Park Road
London
N8 8TD
020 8347 6060

Menswear
196 Upper Street
London
N1 1RQ
020 7226 7076

Buzzing, hectic Islington really is spoiled for choice. This quality store, founded by the gifted twenty-something entrepreneur Ben Sefton Ensdale, offers ultra-hip, exclusive designs in a minimalist, Japanese-style setting. With four stores scattered across north London, Ensdale is clearly a force to be reckoned with. The hiring of the former Selfridges employee Perushka de Zoysa as womenswear buyer-cum-manager has confirmed the fact that this chain has clout.

Clothes are of a very high standard. Sefton travels the world, sifting through the collections of both new and well established designers with a hard-nosed approach and a sharp eye for detail. 'We've already done the choosing…' Ensdale says. 'We've picked the best clothes, styles and fabrics for our customers. We understand them and know what they are looking for – something fashionable, fun, interesting, cutting-edge. Or even just a perfect pair of black trousers!'

Service, too, is high on the agenda. There are six staff, all of whom are given thorough start-of-season inductions into new collections, as well as training in customer care and technical aspects such as sizing. Everyone here works hard in order to meet customers' needs. 'Quite often', Ensdale says, 'people will just call and say, "I can only make it at 9.30 on Saturday; will you let me in?" and we do our best to accommodate, where possible. We try and give a personal shopping level to our service at all times…we really like it when customers come in and say "I've got a wedding in two hours; can you help me?" It's a real challenge.' It's this kind of service that draws the crowds. Weekends are often so busy that customers have been known to change in the toilets.

The store offers the usual customer evenings, comprising sale previews, free wine and discounts. Lots of customers have young children, so three day-long sale previews allows for everyone to avail themselves of the bargains on offer. There is an alteration service available as well as 'look-books' of new collections, so that customers can see what's coming next.

SHOP 77

Shop 77
77 Queens Road
Buckhurst Hill
Essex IG9 5BW
020 8505 5111

Seventy Seven
53 Ledbury Road
London W11 2AJ
020 7221 0999

Open: Mon – Fri 10 – 5.30
Sat 10 – 6

A short walk from the central line tube station takes you to Buckhurst Hill's high street, full of clothing independents of varying standards. At the top of Queens Road you reach Shop 77, a boutique that has received much acclaim from locals, celebs and the fashion pack.

Two large windows with a striking display of extravagant, sexy outfits give a taster of what's inside. The black gloss and white matt interior is complemented by a tactile black marble resin floor. Slick silver fixtures are filled with desirable glam outfits that will appeal to saucy suburban babes and Londoners alike.

Staff are easy-going and are mainly regulars who have been roped into retail through their love of the shop. Here you'll find the whole gamut from casual to clubwear for the young at heart, attracting a customer base of teens to forty plus.

Owner Karen McKenzie is a vivacious, fashion-loving entrepreneur, who began her retailing business from a single room at the David Lloyd centre. From buying wholesale on the continent and working a shortish day, things have progressed to demand longer hours and lorry loads of dedication. McKenzie – still reluctant to yield to the demands of shopkeeping on a 24–7 basis has had to restrict her partying to accommodate her new business persona, but that doesn't stop her from staging many a night at the shop in the guise of customer evenings.

An obvious fashion natural, McKenzie originally opened the store near her home town in Essex with a couple of other friends – offering a juice/coffee bar, shoes, clothes and a travel agency all in one. However, as of 2002 this retailer has gone solo! The travel agency is now kept in a back room, and the change has warranted a new image. Gone is the turquoise and pink velour kitsch, and in its place a slick black and white interior announces a serious intention to upgrade to high status labels. The newly acquired Prada and Dolce & Gabbana labels are confirmation that all is going to plan.

Passionate about her business, Karen spends a great deal of time scouring for new brands, even when on holiday. Milan, Paris and Spain are favourite haunts along with Amsterdam, New York and the south of France. She visits all the regular fairs and shows but doesn't buy just to keep up with current trends, and avoids readily available UK labels.

With shop number two in the Ledbury Road a sure success, McKenzie has her eye on further expansion.

Sixty 6
66 Marylebone High Street
London
W1U 5JF
020 7224 6066
Open: Mon – Fri 10.30 – 6.30
Sat 10.30 – 6

Since its launch in 1997, Sixty 6 has offered a unique shopping experience – a sartorial cornucopia both fun and inspiring. With the Conran Shop near by and Century Design next door, this refined but hip lifestyle store is in good retail company. For owner Jane Collins, however, the site of the shop has personal significance – she was born on this very street – and the store is certainly brimming with Collin's individual and eclectic taste.

An entry bell allows access into a dark, inviting interior. Space is at a minimum, and the store has been carefully divided up using coffee-coloured partitions. A screen at the rear of the shop masks a discreet fitting room. High shelves display Italian vases from the Fifties and Sixties, while the furniture – some of which is for sale and some purely for decoration – adds a refined charm. Displays of clothing on the walls express the store ethos, which encourages the mixing and matching of eclectic designers to style an individual look.

Sixty 6 is conceptually unusual, and the unpredictable range of clothing and accessories reflects this. It is impossible to gauge what you may find here – expect the unexpected and you won't be disappointed. 'It is so dull to have to do the same as everyone else', declares Jane Collins.

There are four sales staff, all of whom are relaxed, friendly and reassuringly stylish. The size of the shop and warmth of the staff makes for an intimate and personal shopping experience.

Collins understands the importance of getting to know her customers' needs and expects her staff to give honest – rather than sycophantic or sales-hungry – styling advice. Regulars are always kept informed about the arrival of new stock. The age range of the clientele – from mid-twenties to mid-sixties – is unusually wide and is a tribute to the individuality and refinement of Collins's eye. She regularly sources designs in Paris, and buys with specific customers in mind.
The unusual nature of Sixty 6, however, means that it is often the designers who approach Collins rather than the other way round.

SWEET DREAMS

Sweet Dreams
6 High Street
Cornwall Place
Buckingham
MK18 1NT
01280 812 507
www.sweetdreams-bra.co.uk
Open: Mon–Fri 9–5.30
Sat 9–5

Sweet Dreams is one of only two lingerie shops included in *Fashion UK* (the other being Sadie the Bra Lady; see pp. 178–9). Both are quality bra-fitting specialists, and both enjoy outstanding reputations. Selection and service, no matter what your shape, is in each case superlative. Sweet Dreams' owner Carol Tomes has been running her own underwear business for sixteen years now, and can be said to know everything there is to know about bras.

Tome's Buckingham store is small and old-fashioned. No matter. The range of underwear and swimwear – covering every conceivable style from the latest high-tech confection to old-fashioned corsets and thermals – is astonishing, far outdoing that offered by local department stores. Sweet Dream's modest size, too, allows for flexibility, and its good relations with suppliers mean that special orders can be met quickly. Cup sizes up to JJ and nursing and mastectomy bras are available.

After just one visit, customers' vital statistics are added to a manual database, which at present includes over 4,000 names, representing a clientele drawn from all over the UK and abroad. This means that customers can subsequently buy their favourite makes by mail order, and that even a partner or husband can buy a loved one a sexy gift confident that it will be the perfect fit. Additional services include home fittings, alterations, and advice for nursing mothers and mastectomy patients.

Tomes emphasizes the importance in her shop of confidential, personal service. She has often thought about expanding her business, but has decided against it because she would lose contact with her clients and her personal touch would be missed. This is also why she has to be able to trust her staff and why she chooses them very carefully. 'In this sort of business you need good staff', she says. 'They need a magic quality, to be trustworthy and have a good rapport and sensitivity towards customer feelings. Confidentiality is very important because you can't imagine what people tell you once they take their clothes off!'

TCS

TCS
28 High Street
Teddington
Middlesex
TW11 8EW
020 8977 8492
Open: Mon – Sat 10 – 6

LABELS
Anne Storey
Day by Birger
et Mikkelsen
Ghost
Just B
Lilith
Only Hearts
Rützou

ACCESSORIES
Accessoire
Michal Negrin
Mootich
The Jacksons

SIZES
8 – 18

RETURNS POLICY
Credit note within
7 days

This Teddington boutique is a secret that's been kept by south-west Londoners for far too long. No more. Sitting on the high street between an upmarket florist and a stylish homeware store, TCS is a tranquil but fun shop offering an exquisite range of funky, flowing, feminine clothes and accessories. From Ghost to Lilith, there's no item in this independent that isn't, frankly, beautiful.

Owner Jules Winstanley has had a varied career. A fashion graduate, she spent many years working in various departments at Next's head office in Leicester and subsequently for other large chainstores, before becoming a freelance stylist for pop promos in the early 1990s. Freelancing is never easy, and Winstanley also had a part-time job serving at what was then known as The Clothing Store. When her boss decided to sell up, Winstanley realized that she had all the skills and passion to take over the business, and did so, rebranding it as the more funky-sounding TCS.

Since 1996 Winstanley has been gently remoulding the store and its labels to encapsulate a younger, more individual style. These developments worked so well that in September 2000 she enlarged the store and doubled the floor space. The age-old problem of satisfying an existing clientele whilst extending a shop's appeal has here been solved with panache. That said, customers are mainly between their late twenties and early forties, while chic pensioners are in a definite minority though welcome just the same. Women are mainly professionals with young children who come here to 'get gorgeous'. There's an expanding selection of menswear for partners, too.

Winstanley has a natural flair for buying and visits many fairs on the continent. Her current passion is for up-and-coming designers from the Benelux countries, who, she says, offer unique design and good quality at a reasonable price. Service is relaxed and friendly. Winstanley wants to encourage people to play, try on and experiment. Assisted by confident staff, you'll be styled to look so damned glam you'll soon discover that you, too, have a natural flair for buying.

VANILLA

Vanilla
13 South Parade
Summertown
Oxford
OX2 7JN
01865 552 155
Open: Mon – Fri 10 – 5.30
Sat 10 – 5

The charming Oxford suburb of Summertown has a flourishing independent retail scene, including Vanilla, a small and pretty boutique on South Parade. Vanilla may be the theme here – from the creamy-coloured interior to the perfume of the scented candles – but that's about as far as it goes. Despite its limited floor space, this store stocks a surprisingly varied range of clothes, gifts and accessories.

The atmosphere is serene, with abstract mood music playing gently in the background. A multicoloured chandelier brightens the store, complementing a fuchsia-pink desk and rugs as well as a leopard-print bench. Owner Renate Beaumont admits that the store is in many ways an extension of her home – indeed, the majority of the furnishings actually started their life there. 'I want people to feel relaxed', she says, 'and I know that many of them come because they trust my judgement. As soon as a new customer comes in, I know her style and which pieces will appeal to her.'

The Austrian-born Beaumont has a graphics and art background, in addition to her twelve years' experience of retail management. In November 2000 she opened Vanilla, leaving herself just two months to stock up and initially buying from wholesalers in Italy and France. Beaumont clearly enjoys her business and refuses to think of buying as hard work. 'You travel and meet people; how can that be hard work?' she muses. 'The clothes are bought according to my personal taste, although sometimes with specific customers in mind. People, like myself, really want a different, individual look.' More recently, she has altered her original buying policy, reducing the amount of cutting-edge designers and increasing the range of labels that carry larger sizes as well as those offering practical, less pricey clothes. Beaumont has become a big fan, too, of certain American suppliers who provide four, rather than two, seasons every year.

With a rotating staff of three that includes Beaumont herself, there is a limit to the amount of service that can be provided, and having just one fitting room must be a handicap. Despite these drawbacks, however, customers seem more than happy to mill around while they wait for Beaumont's expert attention. Vanilla also has a simple mail-order service to cater for its fast-expanding customer base.

WALKERS
OF POTTERGATE

LABELS
Annete Gortz
Ischiko
Leiko
Lilith
Rundholz

ACCESSORIES
Sophie Bigard
Petra Meiren
Linda Soos

SIZES
8 – 24

RETURNS POLICY
Exchange or credit note
on non-faulty goods

Walkers of Pottergate
25 Pottergate
Norwich
Norfolk
NR2 1DX
01603 618 718
Open: Mon – Sat 10 – 5
Sun by appointment

Norwich is home to a number of independent fashion retailers, but without a doubt the most exciting of them is Walkers of Pottergate – an inviting little boutique at the edge of the old city centre stocking an selection of elegant fashion, accessories and gifts. Now in its seventh year of trading, Walkers remains a charming and unpretentious shopping experience, boldly unconcerned by fleeting fashion fads.

The boutique has a distinctly bohemian feel. The navy-and-ivory colour scheme of the exterior is replicated inside, with hand-painted murals and a selection of fashion illustrations by the store's owner, Anne Rowe. Wooden floors are scattered with ethnic rugs, while an exotic window display intermixes garments and accessories with carnations and goldfish in large cylinder bowls.

Rowe's quirky, bohemian style is reflected in the clothing, too. Colour and texture are key themes for her, and she buys key pieces with specific customers in mind – focusing primarily on lesser-known labels. She sources all over Europe from a variety of fashion fairs and individual designer showrooms, but particularly favours Scandinavian and German design. Rowe looks for ingenuity, quality and durability. Whether it's a garment made out of distressed silk or linen or a pleated, fluid affair, Rowe always buys for 'real women'. Interestingly, it's the most flamboyant garments – the most vibrant colours and intricate textures – that fly out of the shop first. As Rowe says, she and her customers are women with a sense of freedom.

Walkers of Pottergate's customer base (age range: twenty to seventy) is exceedingly loyal and spread not only throughout the UK but also overseas. 'People aren't coming to this shop for a safe buy', Rowe remarks. Customers are even allowed to take garments home on approval and buy at their leisure. This relatively unique concept speaks volumes of the high level of customer service maintained here. The staff is comprised mostly of part-time undergraduates, something that enhances the store's youthful, free-spirited ambience. Garments are altered at no cost to the customer, and appointments are regularly booked outside regular opening hours.

WARDROBE

Wardrobe
42 Conduit Street
London
W1S 2YH
020 7494 1131
Open: Mon – Sat 10 – 6
except Fri 8 – 6
or by appointment

Suzie Faux launched Wardrobe in 1973 with the aim of offering a comprehensive fashion service for successful, high-flying women. On a mission to create a calm, non-judgemental environment offering honest and friendly opinions, the self-titled 'biggest wardrobe in the world' has since grown and now resides in Conduit Street, close to cutting-edge designer Vivienne Westwood and 'hairdresser to the stars' Daniel Hersheson.

First-timers, presented with the entry bell, are likely to feel some trepidation as this promises to be no ordinary shopping trip. Inside, too, Wardrobe radiates luxury and quality. It soon becomes apparent, though, that this is a shop that aims to soothe rather than intimidate. The neutral decor – with the emphasis on beige, brown and biscuit hues – creates a serene atmosphere, and clothes are beautifully displayed, with a generous mix of colours and designs – there's nothing tucked away in the stockroom here! Labels are exclusively Italian, as Faux sets great store by the Italians' mastery of cut, cloth and finish. Five light and airy dressing rooms, each with ample mirrors and framed inspirational quotes, nestle at the rear of the store as does the store's VIP consultation room.

Few places are able to offer such a holistic approach to fashion, beauty, health and lifestyle, and services cover everything from an in-store beautician and shiatsu and reiki practitioner to advice on shoes, tights and cosmetics. Wardrobe will even recommend doctors, nutritionists and opticians. But at the heart of Wardrobe is the personal consultation – the price of which is £250, redeemable against the cost of same-day purchases. During a consultation, Faux aims to put together a capsule wardrobe for the client that responds closely to her particular lifestyle and personality.

The staff at Wardrobe are in a league of their own. There are eight personal stylists here, each of whom has an encyclopaedic knowledge of designs, textiles and cuts and a sympathetic understanding of which fabrics work best for different bodies. Attention to detail is paramount and includes, of course, an in-house tailoring service that ensures customers get an absolutely perfect fit. By arrangement, Wardrobe consultations are also available for men.

Faux wants every one of her clients to widen their horizons and address their preconceived notions about what they like to wear and why. After a consultation at Wardrobe, she guarantees they'll step out of the closet and into the street with new-found confidence and élan.

THE WEST VILLAGE

The West Village
35 Kensington Park Road
Notting Hill
London
W11 2EU
020 7243 6912
Open: Tues–Sat 11–7
Sun 12–5

The West Village boutique offers a diverse mix of exclusive, fun and frivolous clothes. With a successful label and concessions at Selfridges, The West Village is the result of a lot of hard work and foresight by ex-*Vogue* employee Lucy Benzecry.

In the late 1990s Benzecry decided that she had had enough of journalism ('I was sick of wearing black everyday!' she comments with a smile), and decided to fulfil a long-standing dream of opening her own boutique. The West Village opened in 1999, pioneering New York designers and focusing on clothes that were largely unavailable in Britain. 'It was either that or selling British fashion in Manhattan', Benzecry notes.

The West Village recently moved to Notting Hill in order to access a wider customer base. Its new open-plan white interior is very much inspired by downtown New York stores, which tend not to be so pristine and bland as their London or Continental counterparts. Benzecry wanted to create a tactile environment that would almost give her customers the impression of walking into somebody else's well-stocked wardrobe. The decor juxtaposes rawness and elegance, mixing an industrial, urban feel with regal antique furniture.

The West Village prides itself on its striking, non-conventional attitude to colour. 'When everyone does blacks and soft pinks, we go for grass-green and acid-yellow', declares Benzecry, who now buys around her own collection, filling in the gaps with other designers (including UK and European labels). Benzecry is eager to promote exclusive products and will therefore always prioritize exciting undiscovered names.

Many of The West Village's customers know exactly what they want, but the very capable staff are on hand with great styling advice when needed. All are past or present fashion students with a genuine knowledge and passion for what they do, and Benzecry encourages them to keep creative. The results include customized T-shirts and handbags that are sold in the store.

Top-to-toe dressing is available, but no appointment is necessary. Two fitting rooms are situated at the back of the store, along with a lounge area for shoppers and their guests to relax and unwind.

WILLMA

Willma
339 Portobello Road
London
W10 5SA
020 8960 7296
Open: Tues – Sat 11 – 6

Sophie Towill and Sacha Mavroleon are both women who subscribe to the school of thought that elevates the 'little extras' to top-rank status. Two years ago, both left lucrative jobs (in jewellery design and the fashion media, respectively) to set up Willma – an innovative and inspiring 'accessories only' boutique that's home to a mouth-watering selection of bags, lingerie, jewellery and other enticing pedigree designer accoutrements.

The shop is located in an up-and-coming section of Portobello Road amongst other like-minded independents. The minimalist black exterior is enticing, while, inside, utilitarian austerity is offset by an array of iridescent perspex boxes perched on industrial-style plinths, almost

creating the feel of a modern art gallery. Playing in the background is relaxed, funky music, sometimes augmented by the occasional contribution from resident canines, Ziggy and Louie. It's a literal treasure-trove. On our visit, we found delectable antique Chinese fabric bags for £460 and sumptuous cushions with embroidered woollen flowers for £105.

Towill and Mavroleon create an inviting space where shoppers can browse without fear of intimidation and where merchandize is displayed to its best advantage. Preferring to work the shop themselves – from serving to clearing away at the end of the day – Towill and Mavroleon have an excellent relationship with their clients and will open up out of

hours on request. They send out cards at sale time to those on the ample mailing list, and give equal consideration to all, with ten per cent discount cards as well as ten per cent discount days offered.

Willma has an exclusive, unique feel, perpetuated by a policy of never ordering more than three bags in each style. A waiting list for popular items such as their Dragonfly necklace, featured in *Elle*, is not unusual. They aim to have something for everyone and, consequently, have a loyal and varied customer base. Even in these oestrogen-infused surroundings, Towill and Mavroleon have managed to create a space so inviting that men can be found comfortably buying gorgeously lacy underwear for their girlfriends.

Population density and consumer affluence determines the retail market in any given region. This is particularly relevant in Wales and the South-west where there are many limitations. As far as North Wales is concerned, well-dressed locals choose to travel to English cities such as Chester and Manchester to update their wardrobe. Whereas South-west England is an area filled with the numerous second homes of Londoners, who want to escape the big smoke but still do the majority of their shopping there. For these reasons independent competition is low in the region.

Many of the choice shopping areas are clustered around major cities, hence this chapter's focus on Bath, Cardiff and Bournemouth. This is contrary to other regions, such as the North, where independents have been forced to trade away from the high street.

Each South Western location has a particular flavour, with Cardiff and Bournemouth offering a wide selection in young, funky establishments and Bath and Cornwall proving more conservative and sophisticated destinations.

SOUTH-WEST ENGLAND AND WALES

LABELS

Anya Hindmarch
Day by Birger
et Mikkelsen
Earl Jeans
Emanuel Ungaro
Iceberg Jeans
John Richmond
Kenzo Jeans
Moschino
New York Industry
Paul Smith
Philosophy
di Alberta Ferretti
Plein Sud
See by Chloé

ACCESSORIES

Anya Hindmarch
Moschino

SIZES

6 – 14

RETURNS POLICY

Exchange or credit
note within 7 days
with receipt

L'amica
14 Post Office Road
Bournemouth
Dorset
BH1 1BA
01202 780 033
Open: Mon – Sat 9.30 – 5.30

Situated away from the town's central shopping parade, L'amica is known as Bournemouth's best-kept secret. It's a surprising reputation, given the fact that its turquoise shopfront touting the maxim 'Confidence is an expression of the soul' can hardly be described as modest and understated. Venture inside, though, and you'll discover what the hush-hush fuss is all about.

Current owner and buyer, Linda Jerrum has spent almost her whole life in fashion. A model from the age of eleven, and later the manager of a clothes shop, too, her double life on the catwalk and shop floor has given her a unique insight into the fashion industry. She bought L'amica from her previous employer in 1994 and has since developed a younger, funkier look, introducing UK and international designers to what had previously been an exclusively Italian stock. The names in the shop may have taken on a more northern European and American turn, but Jerrum has remained true to the store's original concept, offering accessible, good-quality clothing in relaxed and sympathetic surroundings.

The interior is classically smart, set off by a zany wooden spiral mannequin and a beautiful oak-and-glass cabinet that also doubles up as the till point. The level of service is high. The varied assistants – of whom between two and four are available at any one time – are able to offer excellent styling advice. They genuinely enjoy 'transforming' customers with their honest advice and helpful suggestions, and are completely unfazed by the mention of any budgetary limitations. Bournemouth may not be the world's greatest fashion hot spot, but L'amica's up-to-the-minute collections have won the approval of a wide customer base, from trendy mothers and their daughters to disco divas and mature sixty-somethings. Everybody enjoys the same quality service from the staff.

Accessories include must-have bags by Anya Hindmarch and Moschino, and Jerrum has plans to stock shoes; after all, she points out, Bournemouth is not exactly renowned for its range of foot candy. 'I would have to expand the shop so that I could do it properly', she declares. It seems as if Bournemouth's best-kept secret is about to get bigger.

BISHOP PHILLPOTTS

LABELS
Amanda Wakeley
Armani
Cerrutti 1881
DKNY
Iblues
Joseph
La Perla
Marina Rinaldi
Max Mara
Paul Smith

SIZES
6 – 20
(where available)

RETURNS POLICY
Credit notes for
non-faulty goods

Bishop Phillpotts
Quay Street
Truro
Cornwall
TR1 2HE
01872 261 750
Open: Mon – Sat 9 – 5.30

Owner Zoe Johnson studied fashion design at Ravensbourne and originally planned to set up her own label. However, when a shop came up for sale in her Cornish home town, she was unable to resist its charms and chose a life as an independent retailer instead. She has, she says, never looked back.

Bishop Phillpotts is situated on the outskirts of Truro's busy town centre. This beautiful period property once housed Cornwall's first library, but Johnson has transformed it into two stores – menswear and womenswear – and an art gallery. Six arched windows display the current seasonal looks. The carefully balanced interior of beige, ivory and teal, complete with a chaise longue, is elegant but unpretentious. Polite, friendly staff look as if they really want to spoil anyone who walks through the door.

Without compromising her own up-to-the-minute tastes, Johnson keeps a realistic hold on what her often mature clientele actually need. Her design background, moreover, has given her a thorough understanding of fit and fabric, and this adds substance to both selection and styling. Brand names alone do not impress her. Instead, she stocks the very

best of the range, thereby hoping to make her clients' shopping decisions both easier and more rewarding.

Johnson prides herself on being prepared to respond to clients' needs. 'Being able to listen and advise, as well as knowing when to say nothing at all, is part of being a good retailer', says Johnson. 'A confidential counselling service is merely part of the service.' The store also offers a complimentary wardrobe consultation, paring down the unnecessary, unflattering garments that stockpile over the years and helping, of course, to free up space for new purchases. Johnston no longer designs a full collection under her own label but still produces couture pieces on request.

Johnson opened the menswear branch of Bishop Phillpotts in 1997. However, the high-calibre customer evident in the womenswear store failed to come forward, and today this very Ralph Lauren–styled store is one hundred per-cent branded denim and casualwear and clearly targets a younger market than originally intended.

The art gallery doubles as a space for fashion shows. During a recent promotion of an Amanda Wakeley collection, Johnson exhibited the designer's refined bias-cut pieces as 3-D displays hanging from the ceiling. She is clearly not the kind of retailer who is just looking for the latest fad; her ideal is to let her collections develop gradually and to take her customers with her on a shared voyage of discovery.

BODY BASICS

Body Basics
79 Pontcanna Street
Cardiff
CF11 9HS
029 2039 7025
Open: Mon – Sat 9.30 – 5.30

Owner Lisa Karamouzis opened Body Basics in 1986. Previously she managed Joseph's first Chinese laundry boutique in London but then decided to bring a slice of London life to the Welsh capital. Pontcanna Street – now home to gift and interior shops, hairdressers, cafés and bistros – wasn't such a happening walkway in those days, but Karamouzis's gamble paid off. With three television station studios all nearby, the area has an increasingly affluent and maverick vibe, chiming well with Body Basic's ethos of stocking contemporary, individual lines.

Doorbell access promises an intimate experience, and this is fulfilled by the cosy interior. But size isn't everything in the retail world, and the staff are big on both enthusiasm and knowledge. Once in Body Basics, you can peruse *Vogue, Marie Claire, Elle* or even *Drapers Record* to acclimatize yourself to the catwalk styles in context (Karamouzis is an ardent London Fashion Week regular) and then look forward to a complete head-to-toe service from Lisa or one of her staff. That means complimentary advice on make-up and accessories, a general lifestyle assessment and even recommendations for which shops to visit once you leave Body Basics. There is also an alteration service provided by a tailor who has worked with Lisa for twelve years.

Husbands or partners regularly accompany clients and trust the staff so much that they'll ask for gift advice at Christmas and birthdays. Dedicated staff will not only choose presents for the lucky recipients; they'll gift-wrap them lovingly as well. But the service doesn't stop there. Trusted regulars are allowed to take clothes home to try them on in the comfort of their own bedrooms and can pay by phone at a later date. Some clients are well-known Welsh actresses, while others come all the way from London because they can't find a service quite like it anywhere nearer.

THE HAMBLEDON

The Hambledon
10 The Square
Winchester
SO23 9ES
01962 890 055
Open: Mon – Sat 9.30 – 5.30

Close to Winchester's magnificent cathedral is The Hambledon – a tranquil oasis of fashion, beauty and homeware owned and run by Victoria Suffield. Housed within a spacious Georgian building on the handsome Square, it offers a cornucopia of sensual delights.

Suffield's first experience of retailing was in her mother's store – the reputable Hambledon Gallery in Dorset. There she noticed that many of the customers were travelling from quite far afield, including the neighbouring county of Wiltshire. Soon after starting her own family and settling in Winchester, she decided to bring something of her mother's store to her new home city, and The Hambledon was born. Part of the shop's subsequent

success can be put down to Suffield's own enjoyment of her family and home. Childrenswear, for example, has been a natural development for The Hambledon, as so many of its customers are young mothers. Inquisitive toddlers are cleverly provided with a box of toys, and the shop even holds tea parties for mums and their children.

It's a beautifully thought-out store. Homeware, on the ground floor, includes everything from fitted kitchens to teaspoons, while a mezzanine level is stuffed with a wide selection of natural beauty products. The chief joy of the store, though, is the spacious, light-filled womenswear department at the front of the first floor. A single rail of clothes runs its perimeter, displaying a select range of fresh, feminine casualwear and soft tailoring. Victoria's keen eye in buying has led to a versatile collection that can be coordinated easily. Colourful but muted shades predominate, though with a good selection of neutrals, too. Under the garment hems sit a range of colourful shoes – from Audley to Camper – that will meet every taste.

Staff, under the dedicated and capable management of Lucy Coles, know most of their customers by name and quite clearly relish their work. In this friendly, stylish environment, even the fitting rooms give you the feeling of being a pampered guest in the home of an attentive hostess.

HOLLYHOCK

Hollyhock

25 – 27 New Street
Salisbury
Wiltshire
SP1 2PH
01722 411 051
Open: Mon – Sat 10 – 5

Surprisingly, perhaps, the handsome cathedral city of Salisbury has few designer outlets. Thank goodness, then, for Hollyhock – an elegant store just a short walk from the main high street offering a wide range of designer casuals, chic tailoring and luxurious eveningwear. The simple exterior and uncluttered window display reflect the modest homely tone of the interior. Neutral shades of brown and beige provide a fitting backdrop for the classic-driven ethos that prevails here. This is no sparsely stocked boutique, however, and enlisting the help of the friendly staff to guide you through is advisable. A private area at the rear of the store accommodates two fitting rooms, complete with camisoles and shoes.

Owner Annie Brockelbank is herself a former customer of the store, having been unable to resist buying the store when it came on the market some ten years ago. Because she spends as much time as possible in the store, Brockelbank has developed an intimate knowledge of her customers' needs and tastes. The atmosphere is very relaxed, and shopping there is clearly a pleasure for the clientele, some of whom travel from Cornwall and South Wales to shop here.

Customer loyalty is paramount, and start-of-season previews of collections and out-of-hours appointments help to maintain this. There is also a request book for those clients who want out-of-stock items, while in summer customers are enticed out into the garden to enjoy tea or even a glass of wine. Brockelbank's aim is to provide 'beautiful clothing in an easy pleasurable atmosphere'. In terms of her buying policy, Brockelbank is loyal to brands with enduring qualities. 'You'd be surprised at the continuing popularity of a string of pearls…', she declares with a smile.

JAQ

JAQ
16 Margaret's Buildings
Bath
BA1 2LP
01225 447 975
Open: Mon – Sat 10 – 6
except Thurs 10 – 8

JAQ is situated close to Bath's magnificent Royal Crescent, setting the tone for this sophisticated designer outlet housed in a Grade I-listed building in an off-the-beaten-track pedestrian strip. Designed to let in plenty of natural light, the gallery-style interior (stark white walls, clean open spaces and natural-wood floors) has all the extras you might expect – vases of fresh flowers, scented candles, contemporary art on the walls, jazz soundtrack and on-screen catwalk footage. Drinks are, of course, readily provided.

Some ninety-five per cent of JAQ's custom is local, and many women rely on owner Jaqueline Brewer and her staff to know exactly who has bought what so that designs aren't replicated on the social circuit. Ball gowns, for instance, are sold on an exclusive basis. Loyal or special customers regularly take advantage of private appointments, where they can enjoy a head-to-toe service. One particular client, we learned, has the whole shop to herself when she visits, but the staff were revealing no secrets.

JAQ is clearly much more than just a shopping environment. Women gather at the shop to meet. There are fashion shows and charity events, and Brewer regularly invites fashion celebrities such as Lulu Guinness to come and talk in the store. Through sheer hard work and natural effervescence, Brewer has deserved her success. She recently compiled a stylish pocket guide entitled *20 Little Places to Shop in Bath*, promoting the local tradition of smart independent retailing.

JAQ also sponsors productions at the Theatre Royal, recently dressing actresses Jane Asher and Maureen Lipman for roles there. For favoured clients there are even complimentary trips to the latest Theatre Royal shows.

If you've seen it on Nicole Kidman or Kate Moss and you want it, look no further than JAQ. Nobody dresses women at a designer level more attentively than Jacqueline Brewer.

LABELS
Armani Collezioni
Collette Dinnigan
Joseph Azagury
Laura Urbanati
Margaret Howell
Marion Foale
Michael Kors
Rachel Robarts
Sass & Bide

SOLE RETAILER
Christa Davies

ACCESSORIES
Angela Hale
L'Artisan Parfumeur
Converse
Gina
Johnny Loves Rosie
Lulu Guinness

SIZES
8 – 16

RETURNS POLICY
Credit note, with
receipt and at
manager's discretion

PUSSY GALORE

LABELS
Arrogant Cat
Catwalk Collection
Dawn Stretton
Fornarina
Gotham Angels
Kal Kaurai
Kevan Jon
Macbeth
Peter Golding
Sticky Fingers
Tortoise

ACCESSORIES
Mikey

SIZES
8–14

RETURNS POLICY
Exchange or credit
note within 7 days

Pussy Galore
18 High Street Arcade
Cardiff
CF10 1BB
029 2031 2400
Open: Mon–Sat 10–5.30
Sun 11–4
(summer and Christmas period only)

The success of a shop can often hinge on the magic words 'location, location, location'. By setting their business in a busy shopping arcade in the middle of a large student population, a thriving club scene and new housing developments, husband-and-wife team Dax Rodgers and Sophie Gudgeon have hit on a winner. As the name suggests, Pussy Galore used to be very funky and clubby. Today, however, the shop has set itself a different mission, offering its youthful clientele a blend of girlie sophistication and notice-me styling.

The shop windows are an important draw, and Rodgers and Gudgeon change them every few days. The interior is heavy on feminine hues, with a funky combination of turquoise, cerise and silver trimmings. Although small – about 45m² (500ft²), spread over two floors – Pussy Galore definitely has a wow factor, with a blend of expert interior design and funky threads making this oh-so-stylish fashion emporium a complete haven for Cardiff's discerning younger market. Older sisters and mothers, however, will be drawn to the upper floor, where turquoise wood floors, mauve walls, silver circular mirrors and contemporary furniture provide a fitting background for the more expensive ranges on offer, including Dawn Stretton, Turquoise, Kevan Jon and Kal Kaurai. All labels are exclusive to Pussy in Cardiff.

The four main areas Pussy now covers are: eveningwear for the eighteen-to-thirty bracket; daywear (including urban casual, denims, cords and floral prints); clubwear (including sexy dresses and trouser suits) and finally bridalwear. The last also includes outfits to wear to weddings – a gold mine for fashion-savvy teens and twenty-somethings who often find it hard to get something funky yet smart for special occasions.

Richmond Classics
Yelverton Road
Bournemouth
BH1 1DF
01202 295 298
Open: Mon – Sat 10 – 6

Just off Bournemouth's high street, in an unlikely location adjacent to Spearmint Rhino's 'Gentlemen's Club', is Richmond Classics, a stylish establishment selling the latest clubwear and denim labels to a young and trendy crowd. Nick Haynes and Keith McNickel opened this, the newest addition to their growing retail stable, in 1999. Another branch in rural Salisbury, proves that these savy retailers know how to concoct a winning formula.

Richmond Classic's exterior sandstone walls are reminiscent of a department store, but the spacious interior, with its bright purple-and-yellow walls and zany cast-iron fixtures and furniture, is pure funk heaven for sexy singletons, fashion-conscious young mums and trendy toddlers alike. Modern chandeliers hang from the high ceiling, and glass-brick divides create the various clothing sections. The fitting rooms are shower cubicles and come complete with 'showerhead' lights,

though be warned: there are no doors, and no mirrors inside, so you will have to venture outside to view yourself.

The childrenswear section is a particular delight. Fun fittings and special pint-size changing rooms with low door handles and hooks are thoughtful features, but the crèche is a lifesaver. This fenced-off area is equipped with toys, a see-saw, kids' furniture and a television – everything, in fact, to keep the children happy while you get down to some serious shopping. The atmosphere is relaxed and customers are free to browse. On display are up-to-the-minute designs – young, funky and brand-oriented – with an especially generous range of jeans. Sales staff – stylish sirens every one – are on hand to help you.

SHOON

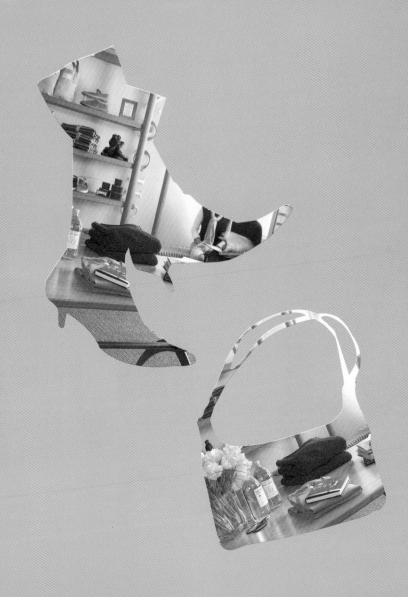

Shoon
14 Old Bond Street
Bath
BA1 1BP
01225 480 095
Mon – Sat 9.30 – 6
Sun 11 – 5

Occupying a prime retail space in a busy pedestrian strip at the heart of Bath, Shoon is the flagshop lifestyle store for a well received chain of shoe stores. Carrying a huge range of outdoor wear, accessories, gadgetry, toys and gifts, this is destination shopping at its best. The popularity of the store is testament to the business acumen of owners Rosalie and Michael Fiennes.

Spread over three floors of a listed Georgian building, the store was completely stripped and renovated in an ambitious but sympathetic conversion costing £1 million. Outside, two imposing bay windows flank a wide central doorway, while the spacious 280m² (3,000ft²) interior has striking tomato-red and green sea-grass matting throughout. Owing to the strict planning regulations, there's no lift, but staff are more than happy to help customers out by carrying pushchairs up the impressive central staircase of stone, steel and glass. Similarly grandiose is the Italian-made lamp-post that stretches the full height of the two lower floors.

The store delivers its blend of quality practical clothing with near-Germanic efficiency. There are simply too many specialist ranges for us to reference in our limited listing, but names like Quicksilver and White Stuff give a taster of what you can expect. The relaxed, laid-back style is pure LA, and the customer feedback forms on every counter proclaim the importance given to service. There are even customer evenings where regulars can air their views about the store. Staff, casually dressed in jeans, fleeces and shirts, are friendly and knowledgeable – the result of careful selection and training.

In case you're wondering, the third floor is home to Café Shoon – now one of busiest cafés in Bath. On Saturdays, tables spill out on to the street below, adding to the buzz and excitement of this excellent flagship store.

SQUARE

Square
4 – 7 Shires Yard
Milsom Street
Bath
BA1 1BZ
01225 464 997
Open: Mon – Sat 9.30 – 6
Sun (call to confirm)

Over a period of twenty years, Square has built up a word-of-mouth reputation as one of the UK's leading independent women's designer stores. Located at the very heart of Bath in the exclusive Shires Yard arcade, Square is now doubled in size, with shoes and accessories housed in a second store across the main walkway. Owners and managers are John McNulty and Lynn Gardner.

The larger of the two interiors is a minimalist mix of glass, stainless steel and concrete, while the smaller accessories store offers a more clinical backdrop for the luxurious stock on show.

Collections are only taken if Gardner and McNulty instinctively feel that designs are right for their customers. Diane von Furstenberg dresses were predictably big sellers, and Chloé trousers were so well cut that they could have shifted many more. But exclusivity is the key here, so Gardner buys only small runs and nothing is bought because everyone else is buying it. That said, there are always must-have items, and both can spot a best-seller after two decades in the business. As with all good stores, buying is often done with specific customers in mind. Two Chloé coats at £3,000 each, bought for two particular clients, were admittedly a bit of a gamble, but both women ended up buying them. Media types, professionals and local celebrities make up the main customer base.

Perhaps it's the excitement of ending up nearly naked in one of the spacious changing rooms that adds an extra frisson to a Square shopping affair…staff believe in trying on – not all garments are best viewed on the hanger. Staff are paid on a non-commission basis, so the truth-and-nothing-but is what you will get if that is what you want. Sales staff, immaculately attired in Earl jeans and Joseph jumpers, are happy to provide appointment-style attention if required. And if you become a favoured client, you can enjoy an off-site presentation in your hotel suite or home. It just doesn't get better than that, does it?

Square Spots
70a Eastgate
Cowbridge
Mid Glamorgan
CF71 7AB
01446 773 776
Open: Mon–Sat 10–5.30
sometimes till 6 on Sat

Occupying a 250-year-old listed building in the Welsh market town of Cowbridge, this intimate, characterful boutique is owned by former window-dresser Debbie Buckley. Fashion runs in the family, with Buckley taking over the business from her mother, a millinery designer. She is passionate about her work, but admits to having weathered the whole gamut of retailing's highs and lows. 'You have to love it to make a success of this business', she says.

The interior of Square Spots, with its dark parquet flooring, old wooden beams, stone alcoves and subtle lighting, is compact, even bijou. Unobtrusive background music comes courtesy of the Costes Hotel DJ in Paris, where Buckley stays during the French capital's Fashion Week.

It's the chilled atmosphere that's the real delight here, though. All four of the sales staff are ex-customers, and a visit to the shop can feel a bit like popping round to your best friend's to raid her designer wardrobe. Buckley is happy to open the shop after hours for special customers, and there's a tailoring service so that clients get the right fit. Buckley often buys garments with specific customers in mind and is confident about what will sell as a result. The stock is mainly youthful and trendy, although there are plenty of classic pieces as well. Happening daughters and fashion-conscious mums could happily shop here together. Stock is plentiful, too, but only a small selection is put out at any one time, so exclusivity is assured.

Customers range in age from eighteen to fifty and come from all over Wales. Recent happy shoppers include the 2001 Welsh Woman of the Year, who bought a Missoni evening dress to wear at the televized awards ceremony; a sprinkling of operatic divas for whom Erikson Beamon's glamorous jewellery is the latest must-have to wear on stage, and the occasional television actress keen to be seen sporting the latest looks.

WILLY'S

Willy's
24 Gandy Street
Exeter
EX4 3LS
01392 256 010
www.willysfashion.co.uk
Open: Mon – Sat 9.30 – 5.30

On a cobbled side street, away from Exeter's main shopping street, is Willy's – home to all things marvellous for those lucky enough to live in the sunny south-west. When owner Suzie Jackson first opened Willy's some sixteen years ago, she rather flippantly named the shop after her pet dog because it happened to be next door to a pâtisserie called Fanny's. The humorous name may have stuck, but the store is a seriously good fashion destination none the less.

Inside, the shop is a little worse for wear, but this is all part of the decor's laid-back, carefree charm, typified at its best in the astrological painted ceiling and the angelic tiled counter. The whole store basks in the glow of its mellow owner, who bestows honest fashion advice on all comers, whether it's a question of a possible purchase or a new haircut. Jackson is also the shop's sole buyer. Her preference is for inspirational, quality design, and all the labels in the shop are exclusive to Willy's in Exeter. The three fitting rooms may be on the bijou side – customers have to step outside to view themselves in their full glory in the faux-bronze framed mirror – but this doesn't seem to deter anyone.

All the staff are enthusiastic, efficient and well-dressed. Service is attentive, but clearly in this shop nothing is done by halves. Even fashion shows are executed on a grand scale: twice each year customers can sample the glamour of the catwalk at a local theatre or hotel – as a spectator or even as a model. Customers vary widely and come from as far afield as London and Cornwall and from diverse socio-economic groups. 'Affluence has nothing to do with who buys designer gear', says Jackson. 'Some will eat baked beans for a month to satisfy their fashion hunger!' Customer satisfaction is crucial here, and, although it's rarely requested, Jackson is happy to extend opening hours. A menswear department in the basement features labels such as Joseph, Diesel Style Lab and Spoon by Pulsar, as well as shoes by Oliver Sweeney.

LABELS
Calvin Klein
Bruuns Bazaar
Day by Birger
et Mikkelsen
Dolce & Gabbana
Diesel Style Lab
DKNY
Earl Jeans
Finn
Ghost
Jean Paul Gaultier
Juicy Couture
Maharishi
Nicole Farhi
Oliver Sweeney
Paul Smith
Philosophy
di Alberta Ferretti
See by Chloé

ACCESSORIES
L'Autre Chose
Ally Cappellino
Dolce & Gabbana
Elva Robbins
Gucci
Philip Treacy
Schwarzkopf Crystal
Storm

SIZES
8−14

RETURNS POLICY
Refund or exchange at
manager's discretion

121

The most obvious conclusion after perusing this region is the unfortunate lack of choice in what is after all central England. The biggest city in the region – Birmingham – has very little in the way of notable independents, the majority favouring a site in affluent Solihull. This pattern continues even in the aftermath of the Touchwood Shopping Centre. This spectacular building, housing notable multiples is unable to compete however with the specialist approach offered by the selection of independents listed within the next few pages.

The women who shop in this area, tend to be a mix of footballers' wives and skilled professionals, stores therefore favour youthful Italian and British labels.

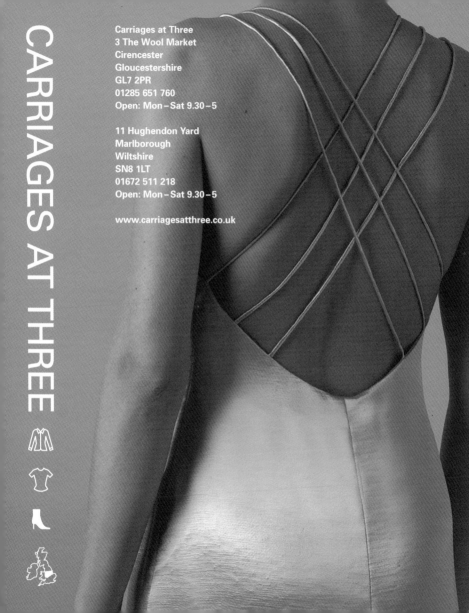

CARRIAGES AT THREE

Carriages at Three
3 The Wool Market
Cirencester
Gloucestershire
GL7 2PR
01285 651 760
Open: Mon – Sat 9.30 – 5

11 Hughendon Yard
Marlborough
Wiltshire
SN8 1LT
01672 511 218
Open: Mon – Sat 9.30 – 5

www.carriagesatthree.co.uk

LABELS
After 6
Amanda Wakeley
Attire
Consortium
Ellinette
Godske
John Charles
JS Collections
Lewis Henry
Lipsy
Mon Chèrie
Serenade
Tadashi

ACCESSORIES
About Face
Mikey
Ray Fife

SIZES
6–24

RETURNS POLICY
Exchange or credit note
for non-faulty goods

Given its specialist merchandize, Carriages at Three's Cirencester store has an ideal location – at the heart of a region famous for its summer balls and racing events. Like its twin in neighbouring Wiltshire, it is dedicated to traditional glamour, its reassuring selection of eveningwear and ball gowns providing a genuine alternative to the ubiquitous 'little black dress' scenario.

Situated in a market square amongst other independents, Carriages presents two spectacular windows of contemporary and elegant eveningwear. The carefully dressed mannequins, however, give no hint of the wealth of collections inside. Owner Rosemarie Watson boasts almost one thousand different styles in each store: 'If you are size 6 to 26, over the age of 13, and have a budget over £100, then you'll find no wider selection of special occasionwear available.'

Customers may initially find the choice overwhelming, but the very friendly staff are ready to help you – providing, that is, you take them up on the offer of a coffee and a chat about your needs on one of the store's comfortable sofas. Shop managers Glenis Goldsworthy's and Sandy Flecher's seemingly instinctive knowledge of their stock and how it will work with individual body shapes allows them to guide customers through the selection process, without being intrusive or condescending.

Watson's policy is all-inclusive: 'Cater for the masses – as many sizes, styles, ages and budgets possible'. Her buying, however, is informed by experience and a strong dose of realism. 'Real women can often be quite lumpy – not everyone has the figure of Britney Spears!', she laughs. The store stocks a number of one-off dresses in mid-sizes 10–12, and with enough notice clients can commission these styles in larger sizes.

Watson's choices range from the classical silk or satin gowns to more overblown contemporary pieces – think meringue, Miami or Christmas trees with flashing lights. She sources talent from fairs such as Pure and regularly visits showrooms in London. Although there are children's toys in the shop, Watson still believes that if possible such an important purchase should be made without any distractions.

There are four fitting rooms and a selection of shoes to help effect the finished look. There is a small charge for alterations, which can often be quite complex. It is worth taking note that there is a sale rail all year round, with items starting at just £50. Accessories include a fabulous selection of shawls (worn with a black dress these alone would instantly make a stunning outfit), costume jewellery by Ray Fife, About Face and Mikey, and even a selection of masks.

Watson sums up her particular area of retail succinctly: 'You're not buying a dress, you're buying an emotion. When women come to me, they often have a worried look on their face and are under pressure to shine at a special event. I see it as my job to remove the pressure and return the smile!'

JANE YOUNG

Jane Young
7 & 10 Chain Lane
Newark
Nottinghamshire
NG24 1AU
01636 703 511
www.jane-young.co.uk
Open: Mon – Sat 9.30 – 5.30

The beautiful castle town of Newark is home to Jane Young – another long-standing store that offers time-honoured consistency in quality customer service. The store is the main occupant of a cobblestone alley tucked away off the town's marketplace. The main building – a two-storey giant, stocking reliable and conservative German, Italian and British names – is complemented by the smaller boutique-style outlet opposite, which dispenses a younger, fresher range aimed at the thirty-something market. The owners and buyers are mother and daughter Janet and Jane Young.

The white and bottle-green exterior of the main building features several highly manicured window displays. Once inside, the Tudor beams, low ceilings and rust carpet give a grand yet cosy feel. Shoppers try on the latest must-haves in one of nineteen fitting rooms, which come complete with generous hanging space, chairs and even boxes of tissues. Partners, meanwhile, can relax: comfortable wicker furniture, endless supplies of coffee, and a good stock of newspapers and magazines make shopping a pleasure for even the most grudging of companions!

Jane Young is a family affair that began sixty years ago as a market stall. Grandmother Young designed made-to-measure and ready-to-wear pieces, and grandfather Young sold them. As soon as their daughter Janet entered the business aged fifteen, it was clear that the business was going to fall into a safe pair of hands, as she quickly picked up her mother's passion for fashion and her father's financial acumen. These days, you'll usually find both daughter and granddaughter in the store, working hard to ensure the family business lives on for another generation.

Jane Young promotes great service with good value for money, with various price points to accommodate everyone's budget. Staff are constantly on the move, running to and from the basement with new stock, keeping up with the demand from the customers, both in-store and those calling from home. Senior staff set the pace, working best under pressure, and displaying a reassuring knowledge of the trade, from cut to cloth.

The bond between customers and staff is close. Clients can spend a whole day with an allocated member of staff and expect head-to-toe treatment. Staff will select capsule wardrobes to meet a specific client's tastes or suggest outfits for special occasions. On one occasion, a customer requested an outfit that would be suitable 'for the Palace'. Staff immediately and perhaps hastily assumed she meant the local theatre, which at the time was showing a Ken Dodd special. A rapid re-evaluation had to take place when it was realized that the client's actual intention was to fulfil an invitation issued by the Queen! Needless to say, Jane Young could have supplied the perfect outfit for both occasions.

KATHERINE DRAISEY

LABELS
Bellville Sassoon
Ben de Lisi
Beppe Bondi
Betsey Johnson
Bleu Blanc Rouge
Caroline Charles
Clips & Caloma
Escada
Gabi Lauton
Jenny Packham
La Perla
Laura Biagiotti
M.A.G. Cashmere
Maria Grazia Severi
Paddy Campbell
Paul Smith

SIZES
6–20

RETURNS POLICY
No exchanges

Katherine Draisey
58 Drury Lane
Solihull
West Midlands
B91 3BH
0121 704 2233
www.katherinedraisey.com
Open: Mon – Fri 9.30 – 5
Sat 10 – 5

Solihull is one of the most affluent areas of England, so it is perhaps unsurprising that it should be home to this jewel of independent retailing – the elegant, progressive and stylish Katherine Draisey. The store's owners are sisters Pam and Kay Cartwright, who each have more than forty years of experience in the business. The shop attracts mainly professional women in their twenties and thirties, who flock here for its relaxed environment, inimitable service and impeccable style.

The window display is classic and light, the minimalist, lemon-coloured interior elegant and spacious. On the ground floor are sparingly selected pieces by high-quality contemporary designers, while the top floor displays a year-round collection of beach- and swimwear – perfect for the shop's affluent, holiday-loving clientele. Stock features an equal ratio of British and European, and male and female, designers, but whatever the sisters buy, their mission is always to source garments that are new and exciting.

The Cartwrights' particular point of pride is the shop's polished and intimate service. They keep a log of what their regulars buy and often buy in a garment with a particular customer in mind. They consider customer evenings – usually the standard feature of high-class womenswear retailing – too general in nature and prefer to make individual home appointments outside shop hours. Staff are chosen for their sophistication and restraint, and are trained for a whole year to reach the exacting standards the sisters require. It is the quality of service, after all, that draws clients from all over the country – and sometimes from overseas – for their seasonal 'retail fix'.

Quality far outweighs brand loyalty when it comes to this store's priorities, however, customer trends are of key importance. Milder British weather, the popular use of private over public transport, and globe-trotting customers have resulted in the summer season covering nine months of the fashion year, with winter coats a thing of the past.

MADELEINE ANN

Madeleine Ann
45 Drury Lane
Solihull
West Midlands
B91 3BP
0121 704 9454
Open: Mon – Sat 9.30 – 5.30

Madeleine Ann is a small independent chain of stores covering the Midlands. There are branches in Leamington Spa, Worcester, Birmingham, Stratford and Wolverhampton, with its flagship store in Solihull featuring in this review. All of the stores offer quality design and superlative service.

The Eighties-inspired, chocolate-coloured exterior of the Solihull branch is inviting, while inside is all black-and-white elegance, complete with marble and mirrored fixtures. In the middle of the ground floor, a couch offers shoppers a chance to relax and peruse the shop's enticing range of accessories, displayed on the surrounding glass-topped tables.

Owner and buyer Madeleine Leddington opened the first store almost thirty-five years ago, graduating quickly from childrens- to womenswear. Despite the well-known difficulties of being involved in independent retailing, Leddington lives and thrives on fashion.

She is the first to admit, however, that the chain is far from being a one-woman show, as Leddington enjoys the support of an exceptional staff. Whether endowed with a high level of fashion-consciousness or an innate sense of style, every member of the sales team delivers excellent advice. It is not unusual for a staff member to spend as long as three hours with a single customer. An interest-free account card will probably speed – as it certainly smoothes – the progress from hanger to till, however.

Italian brands are given pride of place in the store. Quality, elegant and sometimes dramatic design is something that still excites Leddington. The fitting rooms may be basic, but elsewhere the detail put into the branding of the store – on everything from carrier bags to tissue paper – is super-slick.

The service at Madeleine Ann goes beyond the shop floor, however – a capsule collection can be delivered directly to a customer's door for her to try on and purchase in the comfort of her own home. With fellow independent retailer Katherine Draisey situated just across the street, Madeleine Ann is another reason why Solihull has become a popular destination for Midlands women in search of the exceptional.

SCOTNEY'S FOR WOMEN

Scotney's for Women
132 London Road
Leicester
Leicestershire
LE2 1EB
0116 255 9261
Open: Mon – Sat 9 – 6

Strangely located on an ugly arterial road, away from the city centre, Scotney's sits beside a ragbag assortment of estate agents and Indian restaurants. Its poor location, however, simply illustrates its status as a destination store, and for those who live in the city's more affluent areas, it's clearly worth the trouble.

The women's store, opened 1995, is one of three large stores, offering a large range of clothes for men, women and children. A basic exterior and window display gives way to a spacious, highly polished wooden interior with ivory walls and black spotlights, showcasing moderate-to-expensive clothes. Owner Megan Scotney prioritizes affordable quality brands and diffusion designer or named jean ranges. There are also eveningwear collections, however, with a hire service upstairs featuring a diverse range of names (including Ben de Lisi, Bernshaw, Fayaz and John Charles) in sizes 8 to 24. Clothes are sold with a relaxed service, complete with good service and practical fashion advice.

Staff, able to select a strong range of outfits, covering different looks at different price points, varied in age between twenty and fifty. All were dressed smart-casual, but with noticeable image differences.

Scotney places great store by her staff, who are warm, informative and authoritative. Clients are mostly young – a twenty-something crowd of leisurely footballers' wives and young mums with packed social diaries. This dictates sizing policy to some extent, and the demand on smaller sizes is always stronger. Saturday customers are from further afield (Birmingham, Nottingham and Loughborough) and with more diverse backgrounds.

With in-store tailors for alterations, this is a shop that is many things to many Midlanders. Even the spending options have been carefully considered, and there are three choices of loyalty-card scheme to suit customers' various financial needs.

SIZES

8 – 16

RETURNS POLICY

Exchange or credit note
for non-faulty goods

YOUNG IDEAS

Young Ideas
St. John Street
Ashbourne
Derbyshire DE6 1GP
01335 342 095
www.youngideas.com
Open: Mon – Sat 9.30 – 5.30

In the sleepy village of Ashbourne in Derbyshire, amongst boutiques, cafés and a various antique markets, is Young Ideas – a sophisticated, traditional store with more than a streak of the avant-garde. Owner and buyer is Dorothy Thomas.

The stylish ivory-and-grey exterior is unrecognizable as a former supermarket, and the large windows have tasteful displays on metal mannequins. Inside, the wood-and-ivory reception, parquet flooring, metallic pillars and exposed brickwork are very classic, bringing a little bit of Bond Street into the depths of the countryside. A wide range of designers are selectively displayed. Max Mara mixes with McQueen, allowing Young Ideas to cater for a diverse customer base. Tall glass jewellery cabinets are strategically placed throughout the store, holding a wonderful selection of pieces by Angie Gooderham. The substantial shoe department holds the very best in footwear and bags, including Jimmy

Choo, DKNY, Patrick Cox, Di Sandro and Cocinelle. With beige-and-black animal print chairs and dark-carpeted floor, customers can try on shoes in comfort, with or without the outfit to match.

Thomas originally trained at John Lewis, and this shows in the traditional service. The level of individual attention can border on the fastidious and could be overwhelming were it not so impressive. The attentive staff are of various ages, and all are on first-name terms with their regular clients. There are two fitting-room areas, comprising a consultation room, generously sized cubicles, and a communal seating area. There is an in-house seamstress who, for a nominal fee, will turn alterations round in seven days.

'Twenty years ago there were very few imported clothes, not even French trousers', comments Thomas. 'Things certainly have changed.' Now, she says, she sources her merchandize from all over Europe in her effort to find versatile styles for her varied clientele, although she does have a soft spot for Italian design. Thomas puts her success down to her real understanding of her customers and their lifestyles: 'I understand the duplicity of clothing and the various strands of work, travel and family that are part of a woman's experience.'

The north of England has a distinct retailing tradition, a result of the history of manufacturing in the area. Independents tend to be on a larger scale and, in the main, slightly conservative with their collections. Emphasis is, however, put on quality cloth and practical design. Size ranges are broad and comfort is in demand as much as style.

Many locations have had to struggle against the proliferation of retail parks in addition to increasing rental costs, forcing many shops to re-site off the beaten track. This has proved not to be a problem for long-standing stores with a loyal following, but for fresh young shops, starting up and maintaining a business can be more of a challenge.

Manchester is the one exception to the rule. Youth is by far the driving force in this energetic city and the designer garments are more diverse and avant-garde. Glamour is less on the agenda, with retailers preferring to focus on what's hip, credible and fresh.

ARC

Arc
Smithfield Building
59 Oldham Street
Northern Quarter
Manchester
M1 1JR
0161 831 7454
Open: Mon – Sat 10 – 6
Sun 12 – 5

Arc is a large depot-style store devoted to fashion and fine art. The decor of navy wooden floorboards and grass-green fixtures is simple and detracts not one jot from the array of funky merchandize. Arc's original owners linked the store's concept to the rising UK club scene, initially importing US streetwear then progressing to championing their own range.

Over the last five years current owners Ed and Di Matthews have developed the store, expanding the clothing range and putting more focus on womenswear. The rails sport a range of cutting-edge clothing for both women and men, and an abundance of gifts and accessories are painstakingly set out on table tops. Arc's accessories are particularly tantalizing, featuring, for example, groovy handmade bags by Sara Daly. Loud ambient jazz gives the atmosphere an ultra-cool vibe.

The store also has a reputation for exhibiting and selling contemporary fine art, and work by single artists or collectives is hung high up around the room. Every four to six weeks a new exhibition opens at Arc and is a great excuse for throwing a party. Matthews admits that he finds shopping quite boring, and that this motivated him to introduce other experiences into the retail space. Actively involved with the Arts Council, Arc has supported everything from the painting of street murals to performance art and in the process has won many awards. Arc was also responsible for organizing the first Manchester Fashion Week in 1998.

Manager and artist Damion McClung-Oaks embodies the target customer – trendy, friendly and culturally aware. Although the store is undeniably hip and thoroughly independent – with Scandinavian labels and up-and-coming names a priority – first-timers will be surprised at Arc's welcoming approach. Evidence of its appeal is its wide customer base, spanning everyone from student teens to suited forty-somethings.

ATTICA

SIZES
10–14

RETURNS POLICY
No exchange or
refunds

Attica
2 Old George Yard
Cloth Market
Newcastle upon Tyne
NE1 1EZ
0191 261 4062
Open: Mon – Sat 10.30 – 5.30

Tucked away in a cobbled back alley next to Newcastle's Old George pub, in a building that used to be the stables, is Attica – a period-clothing paradise that was awarded the title 2002 Shop of the Year by *Dazed and Confused* magazine.

Attica has been steadily growing ever since owner Stephen Pierce first opened the shop in 1983. The secret to its longevity, he says, lies in not restricting the shop to any fixed period. Accordingly, everything from exquisite Victorian jewellery to classic Eighties clothing are packed into its two floors. The shop is basic and rummage-friendly, with free-form jazz complementing the laid-back vibe. Customers range from teens to pensioners, but the core group is made up of late twenty-somethings.

Upstairs is a huge range of retro furniture, glassware, ceramics, mirrors, lamps and general nick-nacks – all in pristine condition. Clothes predominate downstairs and include an amazing collection of fake furs, velvet jackets and dinner suits. There are two fitting rooms, which are spacious and crazily decorated with clothes stands on mannequin legs and large mirrors framed with vacuum-packed kitsch toys.

Pierce selects only the finest second-hand pieces, from jewellery to hats and scarves to bow ties. Past gems include Biba and Ozzie Clark pieces, but the beauty is never knowing what you're going to uncover. Pierce's reputation in the area is now so established that he doesn't have to scavenge for historical clothing like he did in the beginning when he worked in a flea market. Now many market stall-owners put aside the best pieces for him to view, while house-clearances also prove a gold mine. Pierce is the first to admit that's he's too laid-back to be a good salesman, but his strength lies in his approachable, informative and witty manner.

Pierce is happy to let his customers browse away the day, but is equally willing to help customers search for something special – luckily for us and him, he's a walking catalogue of every item in the store. Whether your aim is to fix up a new home with funky, economical panache, or to be seen in a traffic-stopping vintage original, Attica is bound to come up trumps.

BAL HARBOUR

Bal Harbour
55 Bury Old Road
Prestwich
Manchester
M25 0FG
0161 773 5554
Open: Mon – Fri 9.30 – 5.30
Sun 10.30 – 2.30

A black-and-gold sign sits over glossy aubergine window frames at this elegant boutique in Prestwich, on the outskirts of Manchester. Dark, unpolished wood flooring and ivory walls create a note of sombre modernity that's offset by the stools placed jauntily around the till point, ready for regulars to pop in for a coffee or chat. Paintings for sale appear throughout the store, but the sensuous focal point is a bronze cast nude by Ralph Brown.

This is Bal Harbour – a sophisticated but truly local independent fashion retailer whose owner, Dena Stemmer, prides herself on being acquainted with almost every one of her customers. The store has been open for twelve years, but at the end of 2001 it moved to larger

promises three stores along the parade, and as a result the business has taken off.

Collections are appropriate for twenty- to fifty-somethings in search of alternative designs that are nevertheless sexy, feminine and fun. Stemmer is always looking for new exciting brands, and remains consistent with labels only if they are exclusive to her and keep their standards high. Labels change from season to season, but likely staples include Ghost, Leiko and Natural Wave, the last a range of simple, unstructured linens. There's an exquisite range of eveningwear, bought as and when Stemmer sees something worthy, and a stunning collection of accessories, including bags, scarves and hats. The

stars here are the sleekly sculpted 'hat pack' hats of Mirjam Nuver and Lauren Leleux, which are ideal for travelling to special occasions with and for general storage, too. Jewellery, comprising highly individual, intricate pieces, is fabulous.

Stemmer and her staff create a relaxed, friendly environment in which they aim to make fashion a pleasure. Service is superior yet laid-back. Appointments can be booked, and Stemmer is happy to accommodate those who can't get into the store during the regular opening hours. Wardrobe-editing sessions allow customers to bring in their clothes for advice, while monthly in-store charity fashion shows are a chance to see the latest pieces in a fun environment.

BEAU MONDE

After Eight
by Ronald Joyce
Escada Sport
Guess Jeans
Iceberg
Marc O' Polo
Moschino
Versace

SIZES
8 – 14
(16 for eveningwear)

RETURNS POLICY
No refunds on
non-faulty stock; credit
note or exchange at
manager's discretion

Beau Monde
2 The Weir
Hessle
Hull
HU13 0RU
01482 644 605
Open: Mon – Sat 9.30 – 5.30

A short drive from the somewhat stylistically challenged shopping centre of Hull is Hessle, a small coastal village sharing reference points with a myriad of car showrooms and home improvement superstores. Fortunately, however, this residential haven also includes a small parade of independent stores, including Beau Monde, a lone retail experience offering sophisticated international design labels.

Proprietor Tracey Birkin first opened the shop in 1994 and moved it to its current address in 1999. Having known Hessle all her life, Birkin saw an opportunity, and so, with no prior training or experience in fashion, just passion and a natural flair, she created Beau Monde. Birkin's reputation for consummate professionalism has led to a word-of-mouth advertising campaign, and over the years the reach of the store has extended while the brand range has increasingly become more prestigious.

Beau Monde is a smart, clean and simple boutique, with white walls and wooden flooring. The odd piece of original fine art, painted curtains and an elaborate mirror add a touch of individuality. In the centre of the ground floor stands a glass-and-marble table, with an arrangement of modern artificial flowers. There is plenty of space for access to the garments.

Clothes are arranged in contrasting capsule collections, mixing and matching designers. Funky daywear resides on the ground floor and classic eveningwear on the first. There are two large fitting rooms on each floor, equipped with plenty of hanging space, and an outer lounge for those accompanying the shopper.

The store's USP is Birkin herself – she works full-time in the store and is a hands-on force to be reckoned with. She dispenses bundles of advice enthusiastically and clearly enjoys the one-to-one relationships she has with her clients. A close relationship with a local tailor means that alterations are handled swiftly. Personal calls to tell regulars about new-arrivals, customer evenings and fashion shows in local hotels allow the female contingent of Hessle to experience regular fashion fixes without the bother of having to hike to Manchester or Leeds.

BLUE
LAGOON

Blue Lagoon
46 London Road
Alderley Edge
Cheshire
SK9 7DZ
01625 583 107
www.bluelagoon.co.uk
Open: Mon – Sat 10 – 6
Sun 12 – 5

Alderley Edge is a well-heeled Cheshire village whose high street accommodates various independents, from bakers to florists and Blue Lagoon – a stylish, charming oasis of well-considered clothes and accessories. In her efforts to provide a personal alternative to the local retail parks, proprietor Anna Fern relies upon the time-honoured traditions of excellent service. Her high standards have been rewarded by the high standing enjoyed by Blue Lagoon within the community.

Fern – a former hairdresser – entered the business in 1987. Aware of the gap in the market between exclusive designers and high-street retailing she decided to fill it, and today Blue Lagoon is the most prominent store in the parade, boasting its own womenswear range – Azure – and menswear equivalent – Out of the Blue. The country-style, blue-and-beige decor is accentuated with bunches of hay and wooden furniture displaying a wealth of gifts and accessories. There is also a scattering of chairs and sofas, where shoppers can relax and browse through magazines.

Individual departments cater for a wide age range, from twenty-somethings upwards. Casual, suiting, special-occasion and holiday fashions are favourite destinations, keeping the good-sized fitting rooms (five for women and two for men) permanently occupied. Beachwear by Sunflair and Fluit Plage is available all year, and there are good acccessory collections by Madison Shoes and Pierre Chupin. The basement café is decorated with various pieces of rock memorabilia, including Eric Clapton's guitar and signed pictures of the Beatles and the Stones.

Well-trained staff are informed of stock changes on a weekly basis. However, Fern attributes the true secret of her success to the regular customer evenings where she gets to know her clientele's needs at first hand. Fern also uses the evenings to improve customer service – something, she believes to be of paramount importance. She also studies buying habits using the shop's comprehensive database. The various loyalty schemes, from Gold to Sapphire, and rewards such as free alterations or treats in the licensed café make purchasers feel pampered and valued.

Browse
42 King Street
Whalley
Clitheroe
Lancashire
BB7 2EU
01200 426 293
Open: Mon – Sat 10 – 5.30

This opulent boutique in the Lancashire town of Clitheroe stands out from its competitors. Rather than opting for the minimalist chrome interior so beloved of contemporary retail design, owner Claire Heathcote tries to counterbalance the modernist aesthetic with more grandiose and traditionalist elements, including spectacular crystal chandeliers and handsome feature fireplaces.

The glamorous, hard-working Heathcote opened her first store – a modest one, she admits – at the tender age of eighteen. This eventually matured into a classy designer boutique, which then relocated to the current, larger premises in a more salubrious part of town. For all the grandeur of its design, the atmosphere at Browse is relaxed and unintimidating. Younger customers will also enjoy the chance to 'browse' now that there is a range of funkier labels and a larger denim range, both of which are located on the ground floor. The store team, who cover a wide range of ages, are enthusiastic and unaffected. They provide a detailed personal shopping service and are very happy to take appointments out of hours if necessary. There are specific stylists within the team, but all staff share a love of quality clothes.

One hundred per cent self-taught, Heathcote usually buys with specific customers in mind, as she feels that her own tastes are too classic for the varied women that she dresses. As well as keeping up with fashion trends, this canny retailer also tries to observe more general changes – social, cultural and even meteorological. Nevertheless, for Heathcote consistency in the labels stocked is important, although if collections fail to appeal to her regulars, she has no qualms about abandoning designers until they buck up their ideas. No names mentioned!

CAROLINE BLAIR

WOMENSWEAR
Adolfo Dominguez
Betty Barclay
Caractère
Claudia Strater
C.X.D.
Gerard Darel
Lene Sand
Paul Costelloe

ACCESSORIES
Billy Bags
Guilty

SIZES
8 – 16
extra sizes available
where possible

RETURNS POLICY
Exchange or credit note
for non-faulty goods;
refunds occasionally
given at the manager's
discretion

Caroline Blair
10 Library Road
Kendal
Cumbria
LA9 4QB
01539 730 500
Open: Mon – Sat 9.30 – 5.30

Situated in the affluent and very beautiful Lake District town of Kendal, the branding of this sophisticated and spacious shop has been impeccably thought out and offers a slick and intimate alternative to the department stores with which it competes. Glass, wooden and faux-marble fittings are very much new-age Marks and Spencer, but there are plenty of unique touches, such as the Matisse blue-nude carpet, luxurious draping, spacious fitting rooms and plentiful vases of fresh flowers.

With daywear – both casual and suiting – downstairs and eveningwear upstairs, the store has been laid out to assist the customer in every way and to give greatest posssible access. Designers are mixed and matched, and colours coordinated. Good lighting highlights focal areas, while window displays and carefully considered tableaux of shoes and accessories work as visual prompts for customers in search of inspiration or styling ideas. The spacious interior also encompasses seating areas – where customers can drink tea, coffee or wine while perusing the latest fashion magazines – and four fitting rooms – two on each floor – with seating, pot pourri and plenty of hanging space.

All this makes for a traditional and classy shopping experience. Despite its slightly mature feel, the shop attracts and welcomes a wide range of shoppers – from the sophisticated older bracket to the women-with-children brigade. Something the clients all share, however, is a taste for well-made, quality clothes. Appointments are made outside hours for regulars.

Owner Caroline Blair works hard to instil a sense of almost old-fashioned shopkeeping into her namesake store; to avoid embarassing duplications, she even holds a book detailing special occasions together with items bought. There are free alterations, while working relationships with local hat shops complete the head-to-toe service. Personalized handwritten receipts and a Frank Sinatra soundtrack further consolidate the salon-style approach to service – the type our mothers used to enjoy. Staff are smartly dressed and professional. Blair's future aspirations include moving to a bigger site and the development of an independent department store, with hairdressers, beauticians and a bistro all on site.

DROME COUTURE

Drome Couture
14 Cavern Walks
Matthew Street
Liverpool
Merseyside
L2 6RE
0151 255 0525

Drome Women
3–4 Cavern Walks
Matthew Street
Liverpool
Merseyside
L2 6RE
0151 258 1851

Open: Mon–Sat 9.30–5.30

The Cavern Walks is a designer shopping centre supporting a wide range of independent retailers. Drome Couture and Drome Women, occupying two separate but adjacent units on two different levels, are dominating presences. Owned by Louise Kavanagh and Tim Keating, the Drome shops offer a more alternative selection of designers than the traditional repertoire available at Wade Smith, the nearby four-storey emporium. This is the place for forward-thinking fashion connoisseurs.

The downstairs unit – Drome Women – is strictly for funky young things. The spacious white interior surrounded by multi-fronted glass windows displays a selection of mannequins dressed in the latest cool clubwear from Miss Sixty to Paul Frank. The loud pumping dance music and limited customer service reflect the fact that the teenage and twenty-something clientele don't want to talk. Upstairs, Drome Couture offers an altogether different, more sophisticated experience. With the music volume lowered, both service and clothes are of a far higher standard. Here established names rub shoulder pads with rarer finds, such as Alexander Campbell, Marcus Lupfer, Silvia Rielle and Preen, and the fashion-conscious but unpretentious staff are on hand to help you track them down.

Drome Couture's bright, spacious galley-like feel was achieved only after months of building work, but the effort, the owners say, has paid off. The new interior has expanded the shop's appeal, and it now enjoys the patronage of women of all ages. Designs are sourced mainly from Paris and London. For Kavanagh, unknowns or up-and-coming names are just as important as the staple high-status brands, and the store consequently strikes a good balance between the two. Keating buys for Drome's Bold Street menswear branch, located a five-minute walk away: for smart, funky and versatile styles aimed at discerning young males, this venue, too, is a must.

At Drome Couture, alterations are provided free of charge within moderation, and, in an unheard-of goodwill gesture, if a garment is damaged during wear, the store will repair it and hand it back good as new. One-on-one personal shopping is available, and personal appointments can also be made. The Drome loyalty card allows customers to spread payments to suit their pocket.

LABELS
Alexander Campbell
Amaya Arzuaga
Cavalli Jeans
Dolce & Gabbana
Marcus Lupfer
Miss Sixty
Paul Frank
Preen
Silvia Rielle
Ungaro Fever
Voyage
Whistles

ACCESSORIES
Adele
Johnny Loves Rosie
Pilgrim

SIZES
8 – 14

RETURNS POLICY
Refunds available
if returned next day
with receipt

DROME COUT

FLANNELS

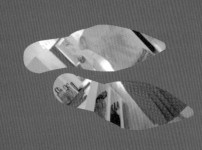

LABELS
Alexander McQueen
Armani
Cavalli
C.P.
Dolce & Gabbana
Fake London
Fendi
Flannels (own label)
Matthew Williamson
Oki-Ni
Plein Sud
Prada
Prada Sport
Replay
Ruffo
Stella McCartney
Thierry Mugler
Voyage Passion

ACCESSORIES
L'Autre Chose

SIZES
6 – 14

RETURNS POLICY
Exchange or credit note on goods returned unworn in perfect condition within 14 days and with receipt; not applicable to sale goods

Flannels
68 – 78 Vicar Lane
Leeds
LS1 7JH
0113 245 5229
Head office enquiries: 0161 931 2550
Open: Mon – Fri 9 – 5.30
Sat 9 – 6
Sun 12 – 4

Other main branches in Birmingham, Manchester, Nottingham and Altrincham

Leeds's central shopping area is now firmly established as the 'Knightsbridge of the North', and people who travel cross-country to visit its Harvey Nichols also seek out the Flannels flagship store, located a stone's-throw away from the stylish Victoria Quarter shopping development. The Flannels Group was founded in 1976 by US-born high-flier Neil Prosser and is today the biggest independent fashion retailer in the UK, with twelve stores sited across the Midlands and the North.

When the Manchester store opened in 1996, the fashion press heralded the shop design as a dazzling example of innovation, light years ahead. Certainly,

Flannels has a minimalist approach to shop-fitting, and the Leeds store is no exception. Its sheer size (1,500m^2 or 16,000ft^2) is imposing, but the art-gallery style is not. Each of the four levels has a different atmosphere. Menswear, for example, has wooden floors, white walls, dark wooden rails and tables in perfectly aligned rows. Womenswear, by contrast, displays stock on suspended rails, floating shelves and wooden tables or inside gleaming glass cabinets. All the units around the store are movable, so that the store layout can be changed once a week.

Despite the fact that the Flannels computerized database currently holds the details of some 10,000 customers, amazingly staff know roughly three-quarters of their customers by name. Staff call to invite customers in for a sale preview or to see new stock. They will also arrange before- and after-hours sessions if requested. Standards of service are extremely high.

Prosser has always maintained a hands-on approach to his job, working in-store and keeping a close eye on every development. His philosophy is to offer labels you've never come across and clothes you've never seen before. All the same, he's not keen to parade his store though the usual channels, such as trade competitions and fashion ads. He wants, he says, the store 'to speak for itself', and word of mouth is his preferred method of advertising. The only thing that is missing here is a fourth-floor lifestyle space with café, art and even more exclusive labels. Fortunately for us, that's all in hand.

GARBO

Garbo
Altringham Road
Wilmslow
Cheshire
SK9 5NN
01625 521 212
Open: Mon – Sat 10 – 6
except Thurs 10 – 8
Sun 12 – 5

8 Cambridge Walk
Southport
PR8 1EN
01704 544 430
Open: Mon – Sat 9.30 – 5.30

Wrightington Country Club
Moss Lane
Wigan
WN6 9BP
01257 426 995
Open: Mon – Sat 10 – 6

Head Office: 01942 272 207

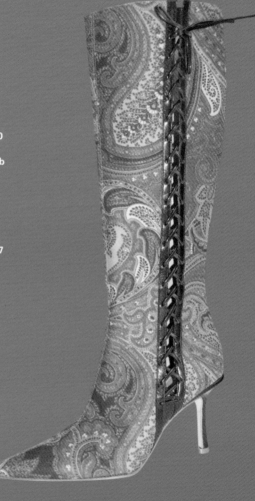

Garbo is an upmarket independent chain based in the north-west of England. There are three branches, including the principal store in Wilmslow, reviewed here. Every store features an intelligent selection of clothes with broad appeal, as well as a luxurious level of service. The powerhouse behind Garbo is Jayne Sharpe, whose aim has been to create stores that are peaceful spaces, removed from the stresses of the outside world.

Formerly a sports-car showroom, Garbo's impressive flagship store – complete with its own private car park and luxury fitness club – is a chrome-and-glass monolith that dominates the surrounding Cheshire countryside. The interior is just as awe-inspiring. Close to the entrance is a giant chaise longue surrounded by vases of blooming lilies, while a central atrium has a moving light display advertising the various and glorious labels stocked.

The clothes themselves are exquisitely arranged and displayed, with the help of mannequins posing languidly from wooden plinths at the numerous window displays. Basics and classics sit alongside distinct design statements. There is a good selection of colour, and jeans harmonize with flashy suiting. A sizeable shoe department offers chic and sexy footwear and accessories to match. Garbo, however, doesn't sell jewellery because, it claims, most customers are already wearing the real thing.

Despite all this opulence, the atmosphere is surprisingly laid-back. Smartly dressed staff are accessible and friendly, and subscribe to Sharpe's no-hassle, no-pressure policy in which 'women are given the freedom to be what they want to be'. Numerous fitting rooms are backed up by three huge consultation rooms for extra privacy. The latter come complete with seating and a rail to hold the pre-selected outfits made on a customer's behalf by a personal shopper.

Garbo is a store that always strives for – and achieves – excellence. If it doesn't stock an item, staff will find out a shop that does. Free alterations are returned within a week. Specific members of staff provide personal shopping services, and there is even a freelance stylist to give edited insights into seasonal trends. A 'look book' is available to stimulate creative juices, and pre-season fashion shows are buzzing social events.

But that's not all. This particular fashion oasis is designed to nurture the whole woman. The upper floor, topped by a glinting glass pyramid, is a place of ultimate relaxation, conducive to the well-being of everyone who steps up the spiral staircase. Here customers can enjoy, for example, a work-out or a sauna, a therapeutic massage or a holistic beauty treatment, or simply just meet friends in the beautiful and tranquil café.

GEESE

LABELS
Ivana Helsinki
Michiko Koshino
Red Dot
Unknown Pleasures

SIZES
6–12

RETURNS POLICY
Exchange or credit note
within 14 days

Geese
74 Bridge Street
Manchester
Lancashire
M3 2RJ
0161 839 3921
Open: Mon – Sat 10 – 6

Geese is a mature, hip and laid-back store offering a succinct selection of chic – and sometimes obscure – casualwear for men and women. On entry, customers find themselves cocooned by a gently lit, dark-grey interior, its chilled-out club ambience accentuated by the trip-hop sounds from the stereo system. Decor, featuring grey moulded-resin tables and spiral fitting rooms, is crisply minimalist, but is intentionally sabotaged by a large vase of creamy-yellow lilies. A warm welcome from staff also helps to break the ice.

Although space is restricted, the clothing on offer is varied. The well-selected collections are merchandized together, and only one of each size sits on the rails. There are no accessories – not even so much as a belt to try on with a pair of jeans – but accessories are not what this place is about. Staff are ready to offer diligent service if need be, but unhindered exploration is also encouraged. Many of those attracted to Geese, after all, know exactly what they want and how they want to wear it.

Owner Steve Caton has a real understanding of his customer base and, after twenty years, effortlessly knows what his peers want. The striking and unfussy garments on parade here corner the market in 'cool' – a perfect reflection of the dress code of the popocracy and the stylistically evolved.

THE HOUSE

The House
69 High Street
Yarm
Stockton-on-Tees
TS15 9BH
01642 790 816
Open: Mon – Fri 9.30 – 5.30
Sat 9.30 – 6
Sun 11 – 4

& Eve
18 High Street
Yarm
Stockton-on-Tees
TS15 9AF
01642 790 343

The picturesque Yorkshire town of Yarm, surrounded by farms, fields and grazing sheep, is the setting for The House. Set in a character building on the wide, traditional high street, this exclusive yet homely store – part of the Steel Group that also has bars, clubs and delicatessen stores in the region – offers a one-stop lifestyle emporium, from fashion to food.

The maze-like interior is tasteful and unassuming. Downstairs is menswear; upstairs is womenswear, consisting of four interjoining sections devoted to a variety of fashion looks. The labels are the high-status brands you might expect – Armani, Paul Smith, Max Mara and so on; however, the store is becoming increasingly adventurous in its buying.

The conservatory at the back of the store stocks a wonderful range of homeware, furniture, delicatessen products and gifts – including a vast range of Alessi must-haves. Once past all these tempting delights, shoppers can reward themselves at the The House Café, where reasonably priced lunches and drinks are served in the café itself, the adjoining courtyard, or, on sunny days, the landscaped garden beyond.

The House's retail director, Kieran McBride, understands the fickle nature of the industry and is always ready to try out new products and services. Sometimes the policy pays off – as with the growing range of furniture and food products by Food Babylon; at others, it doesn't, as happened when The House introduced a range of childrenswear. Experimentation allows the company to gain a deeper understanding of customers' needs.

Staff are smart, sociable and individually styled, avoiding both the conservatism of a black suit and a homogenized trendy look. Training is essential to the company, helping to create an efficient, focused, but relaxed service. In-house alterations have an average 48-hour turnaround and are delivered free to customers' homes.

Two minutes' walk away is The House's sister shop, & Eve, which stocks a wide range of footwear, bags and other accessories, from the irresistibly sexy to the trendily casual. Names such as DKNY, Audley and Pura Lopez are available, alongside Eve's own brand, &. If a customer wants to see how a pair of shoes might work with an outfit, staff are happy to run over the road and bring a selection to try on.

Lynx
20 West Park
Harrogate
North Yorkshire
HG1 1BJ
01423 521 404
Open: Mon–Sat 9.30–6

Lynx Womenswear was founded in 1985 by husband-and-wife team Guy and Morag Hudson. From small beginnings the company now occupies a 370m² (4,000ft²) stylish showroom in the West Park area of Harrogate.

Pebble-quartz flooring and frosted-glass features add sophistication to the simple whitewashed interiors. On level one are shoes and casualwear; level two is devoted to new designers and denim; while level three features a more sophisticated, higher-priced range. Here you will also find a super-stylish chill-out zone, with plenty to read, a cappuccino-machine and a breathtakingly high glass ceiling.

Exclusivity is important to the Hudsons, who spend a great deal of time in Europe sourcing unknown designers. Only two of anything are ever displayed, and three out of four brands recently sourced in Paris are exclusive to Lynx.

The key to the store's success, however, lies in its owners' hands-on approach. Regular in-store events are organized to create a feel-good factor for customers and staff alike. To celebrate the launch of high-profile newcomer Scott Henshall a customer evening was held and even received television coverage. There is an annual birthday promotion in March, and in summer 2001 there was Salsa on the Park, during which Lynx held a Spanish promotion, profiling Spanish names with Spanish wine-tasting, tapas and salsa dancers.

Unusually the seven-strong sales team doesn't include a manager. Each staff member is expected to keep up with new collections as they arrive. During training sessions somebody will usually try on the garments for the others, so that they can understand the styling of each garment. According to the Hudsons, every customer 'is completely serviced when she is with us. We operate a very informal approach so there is no need to make appointments.' Both agree that it is customer loyalty that inspires and motivates the service. 'Customers are always ready for the next thing before you've actually done it. Once you become predictable, things lose their fizzle and people need a bit of excitement. If you are inspirational, you create a following.'

MORGAN

Morgan
15 Watergate Street
Chester
Cheshire
CH1 2LB
01244 347 717
Open: Mon – Sat 9.30 – 5.30

Branches can also be found in
North Wales at:

164 High Street
Bangor
Gwynedd
LL57 1NU
01248 362 531
Open: Mon – Sat 9.30 – 5.30

19a Mostyn Street
Llandudno
Gwynedd
LL3O 2NL
01492 870 817
Open: Mon – Sat 9.30 – 5.30

Morgan – not to be mistaken for the franchise of the same name – is a wonderfully bohemian find, with two equally delectable stores in North Wales in addition to the Chester branch reviewed here. This truly individual independent stocks innovative, rarely seen brands, but the shop's real secret lies not just in owner Helga Morgan's marvellous buys but in the creative styling and merchandizing that fuses designers into a distinct, 'Morgan' look.

The Chester store is housed in a Grade II-listed building with a mulberry-painted front. Inside is a funky interior of Welsh slate, copper-piping rails and sumptuous fitting rooms in gold, orange and black – contemporary features that sit comfortably with the exposed brickwork and beams. There is no stockroom, so the shop is overflowing with designs – unstructured, multilayered affairs with complex fastenings and architectural shapes. Only one of each sized garment is available, so exclusivity, though incidental, is guaranteed.

The atmosphere inside Morgan is extremely laid back. Customers are young nonconformists or original Sixties hippie chicks with a chic 21st-century take on beatnik fashions. All are free to browse, but given the unusual nature of the garments, the friendly explanations and professional advice given out by the two capable assistants can prove invaluable. Hugely enthusiastic about the store and its ethos, these women wear the complete look well and are ready to transform customers into their most exotic selves, no matter what their shape. Morgan also retails a selection of handmade jewellery by Little Women of Paris and Gialle

Limone, the latter specializing in striking pieces made out of pewter and Venetian glass. Such additions mean that there will always be plenty here to enhance your individuality, even if you don't feel adventurous enough to embrace the full Morgan style.

MORGAN CLARE

Morgan Clare
3 Montpellier Gardens
Harrogate
North Yorkshire HG1 2TF
01423 565 709
Open: Mon – Sat 10 – 5.30

In 1997 Su and Martin Allard opened Morgan Clare, a store that unashamedly devotes itself to the cream of British fashion. Located away from Harrogate High Street, the shop radiates an air of exclusivity, its wide bay windows framed in the store's signature navy blue.

The Allards – ex-buyers for M&S – have clearly thought about every aspect of their store, from image to ideology. The shop's heart-felt slogan, 'Best of British Designers for Women', is etched not only on the shop window but on almost every mirror, too. 'British designers just don't get enough support', say the Allards, who nevertheless feel strongly that their loyalty to the Brits in no way compromises their high standards.

The store interior is light and bright. Clothes, selectively merchandized by colour, are set off against appropriate accessories. The Allards succinctly sum up their image as 'fashion without being a victim, and timeless without being dull'. Quality and service are high. Between forays to the fitting rooms, customers can relax on the store's large, comfortable sofas and contemplate purchases as they sip the complimentary refreshments or search magazines for inspiration. Happily, children are also catered for, with a window seating area and plenty of toys.

Clearly this is a winning formula, and the store has recently expanded onto a second floor, allowing for an even wider choice of garments. Only by being very attentive to their customers' opinions do the Allards feel they can develop. Sending out a questionnaire to 250 of their best customers asking whether they wanted a website resulted in money not being wasted on a service nobody seemed to want. A similar question with regard to interest-free customer cards, however, met with a near-unanimous 'yes', and a five-month interest-free scheme was introduced.

Customers can enjoy late openings if required, and alterations are made at no charge for items bought from the current season. Staff, smartly dressed in black, may lack the warmth and friendliness of those of most other independents we've visited, but they are supremely professional none the less. Each season, customers on the mailing list receive glossy brochures illustrating the key looks, with background information on new designers.

OYSTER

Oyster
1 Booth Street
Pall Mall
Manchester
M2 4DU
0161 839 7575
Open: Mon 11–6
Thurs 11–6.30
Tues–Sat 10–6
Sun by appointment

In the heart of Manchester is Oyster – and it's full of pearls. Opened in March 2000 by Clare Hourigan and Caroline Gibb, this is the perfect destination for women who want to buy sexy, exciting clothes by imaginative, cutting-edge designers.

The interior is painted in various shades of oyster-white. It's the small touches, though, that make the shop sublime. The two luxurious fitting rooms draped with pink and silver raw silk include a lounge area for guests and a handmade wire, gemstone and candle chandelier by Dillusions of Grandeur. A pegged back wall allows the store to display the shop's wild looks in a fresh and eye-catching way.

The mood at Oyster is sensual, intimate and exciting. Contemporary dance music plays discreetly, reflecting the laid-back atmosphere as well as the fun, open approach of the owners. Clothes are colourful, quirky and different. And, with Hourigan and Gibb actively working in the store, they can review the seasonal buys first-hand, allowing them better insights for the next buying trip. There are free alterations by Hourigan and honest, funky styling advice from both.

Oyster works hard at marketing itself to the hip Manchester scene and enjoys working with their customers to develop tastes and broaden ranges. Every season the shop holds a 'Girls Night In' customer evening, and there's a 'Wish List' book so that customers' friends can buy gifts that really hit the spot. No wonder, then, that in 2001 Oyster became the winner of Manchester's City Life award for best retailer of the year.

PASTICHE

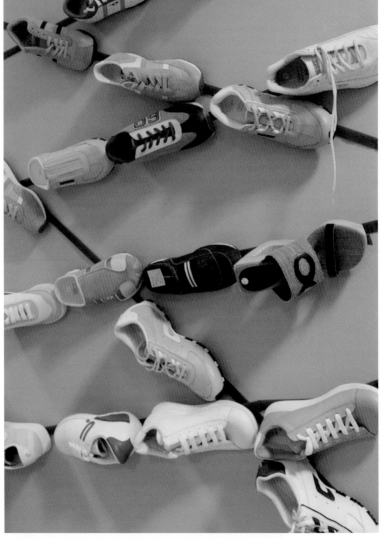

Pastiche
7 & 9 Old Bank Street
Manchester
M1 7PE
0161 832 8595

164 Marsden Way
Upper Mall
Arndale Centre
Manchester
M4 3AQ
0161 835 3230

5 Exchange Street
Saint Anne's Square
Manchester
M2 7EE
0161 819 1614

All open: Mon – Fri 10 – 6
Sat 9.30 – 6
Sun 11 – 5

Old Bank Street is just on the edge of the sophisticated shopping district of Saint Anne's Square in central Manchester. For the last seventeen years it has been home to Pastiche, one of the shopping capital of the North's few independents. Owner Jane Tiller began her retail career selling cash-and-carry stock alongside pieces she designed and made herself, progressing slowly and surely to high-class clubwear. She is now assisted in managing, buying and merchandizing by her eighteen-year-old daughter, Louise. Tiller junior has rejuvenated the buying policy to keep it up to date with current clubland trends.

During the rebuilding and redevelopment of Manchester that followed the devastating IRA bombing in 1996, Tiller decided to upgrade the store.

The result is a luminous white and fuchsia interior that's a perfect backdrop for the growing range of hip and cool labels on display. Rails are crammed with colourful, frivolous and not-so-frivolous casual- and clubwear for teens to thirty-somethings, and there's a wide selection of shoes and trainers as well as other accessories. The upfront house music blasting from the speakers acts as a pre-rave appetizer for the energetic, buzzing shoppers who come here.

This is no market-style fly-by-night, however. The five luxury fitting rooms stretch almost floor to ceiling, and the level of service is very high – an unusual bonus in youth-oriented retail. Staff are selected for their 'bubbly and bright personalities' and are given a two-day taster at the store before Tiller hires them. Their enthusiasm for the store is infectious. Tiller makes a small charge for alterations.

Post the IRA bombing, Tiller also opened a branch of the store in the revamped Arndale Centre, which she uses to retail more mainstream labels, such as Miss Sixty and Diesel.

POLLYANNA

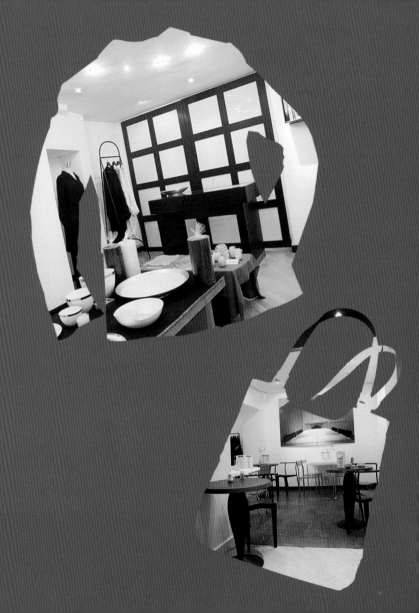

Pollyanna
14 – 16 Market Hill
Barnsley
South Yorkshire
S70 2QE
01226 291 665
www.pollyanna.com
Open: Mon 9 – 5.30
Tues – Fri 9 – 6.30
Sat 9 – 5.30
Sun 12 – 4

Since its beginnings in the late 1960s, Pollyanna has championed modern fashion, winning it the V&A's accolade as 'one of the foremost designer stores in the world'. Despite such an enviable reputation, owner Rita Britton has remained loyal to her native Barnsley, only changing the store's location around the town as it has steadily grown.

The low-key sign and plain doorway conceal a tardis-like 465m² (5,000ft²) of retail heaven. The interior is monochrome, with stone floors, original fireplaces and big armchairs. Finishing touches include classic paintings by Tamara de Lempicka as well as work by local artists. There are lots of stairs in the store, but don't let that put you off – those with wheels or heels can be sure of assistance from the very friendly staff.

Pollyanna is the ultimate must-visit venue. Everything – from clothes and accessories to glossy coffee-table books and gotta-have-it-can't-afford-it quirky homeware – is here. Café Le Croque, at the rear of the store on the ground floor, provides a café-society atmosphere, while the deli service can conjure up a bespoke hamper of exquisite culinary delights. There's even a conference room available for hire on the top floor. For shopping, lunching and corporate mergers, this is the place.

Press is plentiful, but Britton does not pay it much attention. 'There's a danger', she says, 'you may start to believe it. What we buy has to fit the theory of the store, and theory of designers we stock. That's why we don't do twinky-pink one season and turquoise the next. There's a wonderful inverted snobbery in this store where customers talk about how old their clothes are, and how long they've owned them. Every one of us offers a personal shopping service. My staff will book hair appointments for people or arrange for garments to be couriered overnight to long-distance customers.'

Britton is not complacent though and constantly strives to improve upon perfection. She recently developed an innovative home-shopping concept called 'Express Home Selection', which enables customers to access a wide selection of the world's best designer clothes at home within hours of telephoning the store.

Britton is a powerhouse with a down-to-earth take on image. 'Our customers tend to have the same mentality', she says. 'You can't put an age on style. It's an indefinable thing whether you are nineteen or ninety. We don't sell fashion in this store, we sell style – we may be avant-garde, but we display our clothes in a practical way. After all, people have to wear these things at the end of the day.'

POPPY

Poppy
17 – 18 Market Square
Lytham St. Anne's
Lancashire
FY8 5LW
01253 730 826
Open: Mon – Sat 10 – 5

The carpet may be a little worn, the walls a tad too plain and the decor unapologetically simple, yet at three o'clock on a miserable and rainy Monday afternoon, Poppy is a hive of activity. It may not be the swankiest of establishments, but it's the impeccable quality of service and unrivalled collection of unfussy styles for larger sizes that bring loyal customers in from far and wide.

Things haven't always come easy to Poppy-owner Deborah Lawton. When she took the shop over from her mother, she was fresh out of art school and made her fare share of faux pas, ordering designs that were too extreme for the local clientele. Her mistakes taught her the importance of listening to her customers, and she broadened her tastes to offer simple, stylishly designed clothes.

Fit, Lawton discovered, is crucial. Over the years the shop has tripled its size range even as its approach has become more minimal. Adept at remembering a customer's previous purchases, staff are in a good position to advise on the next. Mature assistants, with years of experience garnered from the old tailoring days, share their skills with their younger, more trend-conscious associates, and every one of the four-member team is committed to providing a superior service – whether on a matter of fabric care or the new season's looks.

There are other bonuses, too. A children's play area means that mothers can purchase in peace, while customer evenings, fashion shows and personal phone calls help keep clients up-to-date about the latest arrivals. Fitting rooms are large and private, and alterations are provided free for non-sale goods.

In everything she offers, Lawton's aim is to help even the most fashion-inhibited woman walk away with a stylish outfit. Future plans for Poppy include a well-deserved refurbishment.

RITA VALPIANI

LABELS
Animale
La Confidence
Jocavir
Lauren Vidal
Sandwich
Valpiani

SIZES
8–20

RETURNS POLICY
No refunds for non-faulty goods; exchange or credit note within 14 days at manager's discretion; sale goods non-returnable

Rita Valpiani
50a/54 Parliament Street
Harrogate
HG1 2RL
01423 523 644
www.rita-valpiani.com
Open: Mon–Sat 9.30–5.30

This Harrogate store, housed in an immaculate Edwardian building on one of the town's main shopping streets, is one of the North's finest fashion destinations. Its Harrogate-born owner and namesake's Italian sense of style flourishes throughout – evident in both the exclusive brands on offer and her popular own label.

The interior is a joy to behold – ornate high ceilings, wooden floors and stylish panelling, enhance the elegance and spaciousness of the 370m² (4,000ft²) shop floor. The store featured in a 1979 film based on Agatha Christie's life, starring Vanessa Redgrave, and a certain big-screen glamour extends throughout, including the recent extension, built to house the bridal and eveningwear collections as well as a fabulous Twenties-style fitting room. Stock changes every week, ensuring the latest looks from both established and new designers alike.

Valpiani is constantly travelling to find inspiration, including a once-a-month trip to Italy to catch up on the latest trends. Crucial is the procurement of exclusive-distribution rights on certain lines back in Harrogate, and Spring/Summer stock is bought early to ensure a clear head start on competitors. Only three of the same item are ever displayed, so customers are unlikely to bump into anyone wearing the same designs.

Valpiani's own label of classic clothes and shoes reflects her passionate commitment to quality, originality and value for money. Customization, which takes place on site in a workshop at the back of the store, is an enduringly popular service. In 2002 a pair of customized jeans cost £59 and hand-printed sleeveless tops were a snip at £35 a piece.

At Rita Valpiani, the buzzword is 'individual' – a quality discernible in everything from the range of clothing to the attentive service offered to every customer. The well-trained staff make sure that everyone gets the same special treatment, so appointments aren't really necessary. In-house alterations are free of charge with large purchases, and a ten per cent discount card is available.

SADIE THE BRA LADY

Sadie the Bra Lady
62 Front Street
Consett
County Durham
DH8 5AL
01207 503 032
www.sadiethebralady.com
Open: Mon – Sat 9.30 – 5

97 Station Road
Ashington
Northumberland
NE63 8RS
01670 858 225

33 Sear Road
Fulwell
Sunderland
Tyne and Wear
SR6 9BS
0191 5489 113

Fashion UK is full of exceptional stores, but this has to be the most gloriously exceptional of them all. At the age of sixty-five, Sadie Ayton is bursting with energy and taking her bra business, Sadie the Bra Lady, to new and dizzy heights. With three stores to her name, Ayton – eight-times winner of Butlin's 'Miss She' competition – is upgrading to a slick new image, including a smart new website that works as both advertising and sales-point.

The ex-steel town of Consett is home to the flagship store, and so quaint is it, that it could almost be in a department-store sitcom. Inside, there's very little on display – just boxes and boxes of bras stretching the length and breadth of the store. 'A good-fitting bra', declares Ayton, 'aside from banishing unwanted spare tyres, can create better posture and prevent back injury'. The shop's exclusive bra-fitting technique ('we don't use tape measures here') has transformed women far and near into Sadie devotees.

Ayton is revered as a celebrity in her home town, where she is affectionately known as the 'Quick Tit Fitter'. The 'quick' part is far from the truth, however, as fitting a bra properly takes at least one hour. Customers are consequently advised to book an appointment; the row of chairs at the front of the shop illustrates that there's a long wait for those who don't. Staff are loyal and long-standing, and all are rigidly trained by Ayton, who bestows senior-fitter status only after a full year of coaching.

Although Ayton does keep size details on file, she refuses to provide a customer with a mail-order bra if more than two years have passed since the last fitting. It is, after all, common for a woman's weight to fluctuate, and it's widely known, too, that different brands vary greatly in size. Often customers are not told the size of the bra they are purchasing until they are queuing to pay. This prevents them recoiling in disbelief and horror at a shocking change in their statistics.

The key to the Bra Lady's success is her interest in fashion and women's bodies. Ayton has always believed a good bra should work in harmony with a designer outfit. When she began a lingerie sideline to her clothing business in the 1970s, Ayton discovered that 'all the bra measurement guides were wrong'. She also realized that the quality of the elastic played a vital part in good-fitting underwear and formulated her own fitting methods to ensure a bounce-free situation. Ayton often deals with mastectomy patients and nursing mothers, but turns medical advice on its head. As a firm believer in the underwire, Ayton knows that in a good-fitting bra the wire should come nowhere near the breast tissue, and as a result believes that underwired bras can be safely worn by pretty much everyone.

Like many of the retailers featured in this book, expansion is on the cards for Ayton. She has ambitious plans to franchise her company, but is firm in her determination to maintain rigid quality and service in every store. Her aim, she says, is to fit the whole of womankind with the correct size bra.

SUNDAY BEST

LABELS
L'Altra Moda
Caractère
Joseph
Kyri
Nicole Farhi
Nolita
Oska
Pinko
Shirin Guild

SIZES
10 – 18

RETURNS
No refund on non-faulty
goods; exchange or
credit note within
7 days with receipt

Sunday Best
Victoria Jubilee Buildings
Rawtenstall
Rossendale
Lancashire BB4 8DY
01706 215 495
www.sunday-best.com
open: Mon – Fri 9.30 – 6
Sat 9.30 – 5.30
Thurs by appointment only

The quaint Lancashire town of Rawtenstall is by no means easy to reach – by public transport, at least – but for those willing to travel for good-looking clothes, this jewel of an independent will reward any trouble taken. Sunday Best has been trading for thirty years – though it would be hard to guess this from the smart contemporary decor and the up-to-the-minute attitude of the store's owner, Jan Shutt.

The window displays, set within large grey-framed windows, are elegant and inviting; the atmosphere inside a real joy. Attention to detail is evident everywhere, from the central lounge area to the beautifully appointed fitting rooms. One-third of the ground floor is devoted to menswear – so don't rule out bumping into a fashionable footballer or two from nearby Manchester. The other two-thirds, however, is pure womenswear heaven, while the first floor is home to a permanent sales room that's well worth checking out.

Shutt buys both classic labels and exclusive unknowns. She favours English and Italian designers but likes to forage for the unusual; an Italian label called Pinko, for example, is bought on a weekly basis over the Internet. 'You learn something every day about fashion, and the minute you stop learning you're dead,' says Shutt. She became the first independent retailer to speak out against the excessive prices certain designers were demanding, and today she still bars certain brands from her shop. I believe that fashion should be product- and not designer-led', she declares roundly. That said, she always purchases two or three collections that have traffic-stopping potential, knowing full well that even if they won't necessarily sell, they will bring people into the shop and help sell the other products.

Staff – every one of whom has been individually head-hunted by Shutt – are friendly, funky but level-headed. If you need more specialized service, private appointments are available; Thursdays, when the shop is otherwise closed, is set aside for this purpose. The fact that Sunday Best's first customer thirty years ago still shops here is a good indication of the loyalty the shop inspires. Shutt is quick to recognize the importance of such loyalty, especially for an independent. It can have advantages beyond the till receipts, she says. When one customer stayed to help serve an influx of visitors just before closing time, she was given a beautiful and highly desirable jumper as a thank-you present. 'As an independent', Shutt reflects, 'you can't just shut the door if there are customers still to be served. It's a tough business, and there's always so much more to do…Sometimes I feel I've created a monster here, and I'm just trying to control it!'

TESSUTI

Tessuti
14–20 Watergate Street
Chester
Cheshire
CH1 2LA
01244 400 055
Open: Mon–Sat 9.30–5.30
Sun 11.30–5

With its castle ruins, Gothic churches and half-timbered Tudor houses, Chester is one of Britain's most beautiful cities. Tessuti – opened in 1985 – is a suitably stylish store occupying one of the few modern buildings around, allowing for a large balcony window display. A short escalator journey from street level leads to two spacious floors of eclectic chic designer mens- and womenswear.

The men's floor has an air of made-to-measure luxury, the framed press clippings of Tessuti's in-house football and cricket team victories adding a personal touch to the traditional wooden interior. Womenswear – introduced at a later date in response to demand – is an altogether lighter, airier and more upbeat affair. Stone and white walls and floors are complemented by navy soft furnishings, including a large modern chaise longue. A television plays current- and future-season catwalk shows, so customers can share in the glamour and drama of high fashion as well as glean styling suggestions. Music is current but unobtrusive.

Womenswear is merchandized into three looks – tailored, casual and funky – with designers separated and individually signed. There are luxurious fitting rooms on either side of the floor and a central till point area that has the grandeur of an exclusive hotel reception.

A comprehensive shoe and bag department is surrounded by all kinds of accessories, from sunglasses to scarves.

First-timers have nothing to fear here. Despite the swanky setting, staff are wonderfully relaxed and approachable, even if slickly suited. Covering all different ages, they form a skilled team, offering excellent advice without the designer sneer. Added extras – such as summer open evenings with champagne and nibbles, personal shopping services and an interest-free storecard – also help make shopping here a stress-free pleasure.

Tessuti offers a solid selection of designers. Buying and retail director, Jay Montessori, is aware of the problem of stocking a store that aims to remain sparse – particularly as he likes to take on new labels alongside the better-known brands. 'We want women to feel unintimidated and excited by our stock. Chester is not London, and there are obvious fashion boundaries that have to be respected, but it's up to our staff to put people at ease and help them to try something new.'

VAN MILDERT

Van Mildert
19–21 Elvet Bridge
Durham
DH1 3AA
0191 384 8500
Open: Mon–Sat 10–5.30
Sun 12–5

Situated just over the Elvet Bridge and enjoying amazing views over the River Wear, Van Mildert is Durham's designer haven and includes expansive womens- and menswear departments as well as a basement café and a huge funky bar.

The white wooden front of the womenswear store opens to an interior of dusky-pink, mulberry and white walls and fittings. The atmosphere is open and friendly, with soulful R&B banishing any presumption of pretentiousness. Staff are twenty- to thirty-somethings (a reflection of the core clientele) and are helpful, chatty and fashion-aware. Their ability to break the ice, combined with a complete lack of hard-sell, attracts a wide variety of customers, from students to housewives to older 'ladies of leisure'. In short, it's a refreshing alternative to the aggressive boutique culture that predominates in neighbouring Newcastle.

The womenswear store consists of a ground floor and basement, and features a contemporary range of contrasting styles and price points. A great selection of colours and neutrals, classics and alternatives, is available. Director and buyer, Lisa Cane, is aware that her customers will pay for quality clothing, but value for money is still essential. Menswear is strictly segregated into tailoring and casual, and led by luxurious brands such as Prada and Armani.

Van Mildert also sells luxury furniture, homeware and appliances by Arad, Space Boudoir and Bang & Olufsen, to name a few. These lifestyle products are displayed in the windows, creating an 'at home' environment for the beautifully dressed mannequins also on show.

Scotland is another region where population and terrain has dictated shopping patterns. The cities remain the focal point for cutting-edge retailing and the big three – Edinburgh, Glasgow and Aberdeen – each possess a select number of destination boutiques.

Glasgow is a vibrant city, with a multitude of bars and restaurants. It is also the shopping capital of Scotland and therefore crammed with fabulous outlets. The retail districts are split in two, with many of the downtown independents offering less in the way of service, in order to keep up with high street chains and the busy footfall of irregular customers.

Alternatively, the Hindburgh Road has a great wealth of contrasting stores that offer current classics with an impeccable personal touch.

Aberdeen is a strong contender for the second most popular shopping region, simply due to the wealth that the oil industry has brought to the city. Edinburgh on the other hand, has surprisingly few good shops to compete with Jenners department store, especially when considering the wealth of the population and the influx of tourists.

CLUE

Clue
45 Thistle Street
Edinburgh
EH2 1DY
0131 220 6174
Open: Mon – Sat 10 – 6
except Thurs 10 – 7

Opened at the end of 2000, Clue has brought a much-needed fashion staple to Edinburgh. Focusing on sophisticated yet sexy continental designers, this small boutique retails its range of funky separates and stylish suiting in a fresh, minimalist decor. Spanish owner, Gema Bernad, moved to Scotland four years ago, having decided that the UK was to be her new home but considering London too frenetic to be her permanent base.

Bernad's background in retail had made her aware of the giant gap in the market between top-end designer and mass-manufactured clothing. Clue aims to fill it, providing a quality alternative to the high-street homogeneity that prevails elsewhere. Among the chic and slinky outfits are many labels that are otherwise unavailable in the UK, including Tattoo, A Ménos Cuarto and Coutura. With only a few sizes of each design stocked, customers are able to create an exclusive and individual image. Bernad has also recently added a small but perfectly

selected range of Spanish shoes to her stock, which, like her choice of accessories, complement her clothing ranges perfectly.

Prices are reasonable, enabling Clue to appeal to a broad clientele – both fashion-conscious teenagers and middle-youth thirty-somethings. Except in the summer and Christmas seasons, Bernad is usually the only member of staff but is able to offer intimate service all the same. When required, she can offer detailed advice and information in a fun, friendly manner, but crucially knows how to take a more back-seat attitude when fashion connoisseurs want freedom to explore.

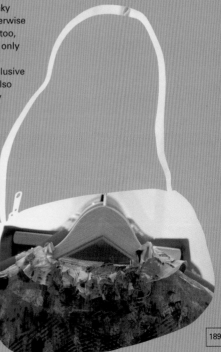

Corniche

2 – 4 Jeffery Street
Edinburgh
EH1 1DT
0131 556 3707
Open: Mon – Sat 10 – 5.30

The glorious city of Edinburgh is home to the splendid Corniche, a pioneer in the retail of exotic fashions from all over the world. For those unfamiliar with the Scottish capital's labyrinthine Old Town, the store can be difficult to find, though wandering through these quaint streets is hardly a hardship, unless, of course, you happen to be in heels. Once found, the simple painted exterior is inoffensive enough, but a glance at the stunning experimental window displays should be enough to tempt you in. Sexy, luxurious, flamboyant 'fashion artists' are the focus for this most passionate of independents.

When it first opened in 1978, Corniche was something of a joke to locals. Owner Nina Grant had begun customizing her own clothes at a young age, and this inspired her to set up a retail outlet with a modest collection of made-to-measure leather trousers. She quickly expanded to include more designer labels, and Corniche established a reputation for championing the radical and new and for flying in the face of 'safe and sensible' fashion. The sculptural creations of the Japanese designer Issey Miyake were just some of those that drew ridicule in those days. Today, however, everything's

different, and Grant is one of the most established and respected buyers working in the UK. The quest for originality is still her raison d'être, and many of the labels on display – from icons such as Miyake and Westwood to more recent revolutionaries such as Arkadius – are exclusive to Corniche in Edinburgh.

There are two stores in Jeffery Street – Corniche Womenswear and Corniche Menswear. At Corniche Womenswear, chic urban style is juxtaposed with opulent grandeur. An elaborate interior of wooden floors, scaffold clothes rail and modern furniture strikes a balance between elegant classicism and high-tech thinking. The focal point is a huge mirror elaborately decorated with a cascade of flowers that stretches across the back wall. Touchingly, Grant's dog, Poppy, can often be found asleep in her basket, unfazed by the comings and goings of Edinburgh's most stylish denizens.

Grant and Poppy are not the only long-standing members of Corniche; Heather MacLennan and Ian Moutter, who also work in the store, have devoted more than twenty-five years of service between them. This guarantees assistance from someone who really knows what they're talking about and who has a love for all that Corniche stands for. Corniche Menswear, next door, offers a more subdued shopping experience but equally stunning clothing. It's a gold mine for men who want to be individually stylish without looking overdressed.

CRUISE

Cruise
180 – 188 Ingram Street
Glasgow
G1 1DN
0141 572 3232 head office: 0141 572 3200

223 Ingram Street
Glasgow
G1 1DA
0141 229 0000

31 Castle Street
Edinburgh
EH2 3DN
0131 220 4441

94 George Street
Edinburgh
EH2 3DF
0131 226 3524

All open: Mon – Fri 10 – 6
except Thurs 10 – 7
Sat 9.30 – 6
Sun 12 – 5

1 – 6 Princess Square
Newcastle
NE1 8ER
0191 261 0510
Open: Mon – Sat 9.30 – 5.30
except Thurs 9.30 – 7.30
Sun 11.30 – 4.30

The Glasgow flagship of the three-branch mens- and womenswear chain Cruise is situated towards the business district of the city, close to a variety of prestigious international designer stores. Housed in a large and rather grand-looking building, this store offers what can best be described as pure, indulgent luxury and is one of the few independents that can rival the likes of Harvey Nics in its ability to put a human face on high-status selling.

Roughly speaking the shop becomes more exclusive the higher you climb (though you could take the lift!). The ground floor is devoted to accessories, with an impressive range of all the big labels and more. The top floor is reserved for the most expensive items, and the level of service becomes much more attentive to illustrate this point. On every floor, however, it's Cruise's ability to offer a select 'hand-picked' range of clothes that marks it out from many large-scale competitors. Fitting rooms, of which womenswear has sixteen, are spacious, luxurious and designed with panache, while adjoining lounge areas enable customers to take stock of their purchases or indulge in a cup of tea or glass of wine.

Service is intimate, and staff are on first-name terms with many of their customers and willing to make out-of-hours appointments, if required. All staff members are trained in the styling of the new season's collections, and all, too, have an input into buying policy. Sales assistants are a variety of ages and types, and are encouraged to bring their individuality to the shop floor.

Cruise aims to be aspirational yet simultaneously attract a wide customer base (hence the existence of a separate denimwear store). Personal shopping is a service given to everyone, even if they can only afford to scrape together the money for a D&G purse.

Jane Davidson
52 Thistle Street
Edinburgh
EH2 1EN
0131 225 3280
Open: Mon – Sat 9.30 – 6
except Thurs 9.30 – 7

For the last few years, the eponymous Jane Hall has managed this elegant Edinburgh womenswear shop alongside her daughter Sarah, an ex-model and a PR graduate from the London College of Fashion. Early in 2002, Sarah Davidson – still in her early twenties – became the sole proprietor. The business has clearly benefited from the introduction of new blood. Service has been rejuvenated, and the store's appeal broadened to encompass hip twenty-somethings as well as the existing, classically minded clientele.

Jane Davidson is situated on a quiet road in the New Town area of Edinburgh, in a classically Scottish grey stone building. A simple black sign beckons customers into the understated, elegant interior, where ivory walls and sea-grass floors form a subdued backdrop to the light wooden furniture, allowing the clothes to take centre stage. A small open fire adds a welcoming touch.

There are three floors in all. On the ground floor is daywear, represented by classic, ageless labels such as Day, Sand and Anne Storey, while the first floor houses the recently opened denim section, where funky See by Chloé and Iceberg essentials are merchandized alongside the desirable footwear designs of Jimmy Choo. Finally, the upper floor is reserved for tailoring and dressier designs by the likes of Clements Ribeiro and Féraud.

The store has a relaxed and friendly feel, with talented staff including the store's founder, Jane Hall, who is still on hand for styling tips. Other attractions include alteration and dry-cleaning services, deliveries to customers living in hard-to-reach places, and personal wardrobe consultations by Davidson fille. One of the latter's most successful innovations has been the monthly in-house fashion shows, which introduce new designs and fashion ideas to her sometimes chary clientele. Nudging her older clients towards a more evolved understanding of fashion has been Davidson's mission: 'We've succeeded in translating trends so they can still look modern yet be unintimidating for an Edinburgh market.'

KAFKA

Kafka
5 Alford Place
Aberdeen
AB10 1NP
01224 626 002

41 Union Terrace
Aberdeen
AB25 1NE
01224 625 711

15 Rosemount Viaduct
Aberdeen
AB25 1NE
01224 625 711

Open: Mon – Sat 10 – 6
except Thurs 10 – 7.30

The elegant city of Aberdeen is rightly home to Kafka – one of Scotland's most elegant clothing stores. There are three branches in all, of which two stock womenswear. The Union Terrace and Rosemount Viaduct branches are geared to more casual and contemporary fashions, while the flagship branch at Alford Place, reviewed here, is a more exclusive affair, offering a high level of personal service and an even higher calibre of designer clothing.

Brothers Russell and David Cameron started retailing clothes more than a decade ago. Initially focusing on menswear, they gradually developed their womenswear ranges as a result of popular demand. In 2000 the brothers were joined by former Sports Max wholesaler Karin Smith as the store's womenswear buyer, and she plans to diversify the range still further.

The new flagship store oozes refinement and exclusivity. Opaque perspex screens at the window partially obscure the interior, and there's a bell to gain entry. Inside, the cherrywood and green-glass flooring complement the streamlined glass-and-chrome fixtures, creating a sophisticated shopping environment. Plush fitting rooms and dedicated lounge area enhance the theme of pure luxury that prevails throughout. Sleek tailoring is definitely the order of the day here, and high-status classic brands such as Armani and Joseph predominate.

Kafka's well-dressed staff are selected for their communication skills and fashion flair. Intense training ensures that everyone is up to scratch on the designs available, current styling trends and even product care. This complete service is all part of Kafka's personal shopping experience, but good service is not just about an attentive sale. As Smith astutely observes, 'Sometimes a simple smile is all that a customer wants or needs.'

People finding the flagship Alford store a tad too overdone for their taste might do well to visit Kafka's Union Terrace branch. Here, the interior of deep purples, muted yellows and pine furnishings is warmer and the ambience younger and more laid-back. The quality of the designers is still high, but the emphasis is on casual and trendy clothing.

MOON

Moon
10 Ruthven Lane
Glasgow
G12 9BG
0141 339 2315
Open: Mon – Sat 10 – 5.30

At first sight, Ruthven Lane looks like an unremarkable cobbled passage leading off the Byers Road – Glasgow's trendy student hangout full of bustling bars and cafés. Explore, however, and it soon becomes obvious that it is home to some interesting places, including an antique shop, a restaurant, and even a yoga venue. Most notable of all, though, is Moon – a modest but attractive boutique that has more than stood the test of time since first opening back in the Seventies

The present owner, Annie Good – a former university librarian – took over the store in 1988. Good had no prior fashion experience, and she describes her induction to the industry as a steep learning curve: 'I wasn't wet behind the ears; I was drenched.' The biggest challenge for Good was the task of buying desirable designers when minimum orders are often so exaggeratedly high. Good has clearly succeeded, however, and Moon prospers as a much-valued independent, relying on word-of-mouth alone to promote itself.

Moon is a versatile shopping venue for women above the age of twenty-five. On offer is a diverse selection of British and European clothing, alongside an exquisite range of delicate, unusual accessories. Scarves by Pazuki, for example, are real works of art. Iconic designers like Paco Rabanne sit with current fashion favourites such as Marcus Lupfer and relative unknowns like Carol Waller to offer the kind of delectably unpredictable collections that department stores often overlook.

Moon's two fitting rooms are modest in size, but the relaxed intimacy of the store allows you to walk around in comfort, using the shop-floor mirrors to boost your viewing opportunities. Service is informal and informative, as Good or her assistant strive to find a customer's ideal outfit, with an honest opinion on fit and style. There has been no need for appointments in the past, although Good is happy to consider keeping the store open late, if need be. Genuine, humorous and naturally chatty, Good ensures that even if a customer doesn't walk out with a bag in her hand, she'll still have a smile on her face.

PAMPAS

Pampas
78/80 Hyndland Road
Glasgow
G12 9UT
0141 339 8860
Open: Mon – Sat 9.30 – 5.30

Opened in 1990, Pampas provides classic, traditional clothing for women of all ages in the Glasgow area. Owners Alice Johnson and Helen Forrest have created an individual, specialist establishment whose focus is on quality cloth and eclectic, understated design. With many long-standing regular customers to its name, the shop has the feel of an inclusive and intimate club.

The store is spacious and light, with the dominant decor comprising ivory and earth hues. The collections on display are classically elegant, including such names as Jean Muir, Sand and Joyce Riding, and provide ample choice in daywear, accessories and occasionwear. The mezzanine at the rear of the shop houses yet more clothes and accessories (sleek hats by Victoria Ann are a particular focal point), along with four good-sized fitting rooms. The atmosphere is lifted by the background music of credible pop and the friendly, open service.

When it comes to buying, Johnson places a special importance on lifestyle. The continued success of the store, she believes, is the result of a thorough understanding of her clientele. 'We ask ourselves where these people are going? How much leisure time do they enjoy, and are certain styles practical or wearable? People are no longer willing to be walking fashion labels, they want something unique and versatile.'

Pampas also has a subsidiary lingerie boutique, just two shops down the parade. This also specializes in year-round beachwear, ensuring that clients' clothing needs can be met come rain or shine.

Swanky Modes
49 Rose Street
Aberdeen AB10 1UB
01224 624 950
Open: Mon – Sat 10 – 6
except Thurs 10 – 7

This modest boutique aims to be the discerning high-street shoppers' first step up the designer ladder, offering affordable, aspirational brands such as Day and Gotham Angels (see p.54–55) to a broad, fashionable clientele.

Owners Jackie Paterson and Libby Bruce have come from diverse backgrounds – one worked in an oil company, the other had her own furniture shop – but each brought equal measures of passion and professionalism to their new line of business. Quickly honed in on the missing link in the Aberdeen market, they use pre-season and short-term buying to create a very current range of clothes at competitive prices. They're well aware, too, that exclusivity is an important part of the designer buzz. 'One of the main attractions of shopping at Swanky Modes', says Bruce, 'is that we don't stock lots of the same item, so customers aren't going to turn up at a party and meet someone with the same outfit.'

The store is refreshingly unstuffy. Decor features relaxing lilacs and deep purples, while dainty drop lighting gives a fairy-tale effect. Both owners work full-time in-store, and service is friendly and

personal. Equal respect is given to teenage clientele and to wealthier thirty-something patrons. Two large fitting rooms are draped with luxurious velvet curtains, and fixtures are smart and uncluttered. Paterson and Bruce plan to expand the store's merchandize. Shoes are a mutual love of both, and they soon hope to add affordable designer footwear to their fun and pocket-friendly range.

LABELS
Anouska G
D.Exterior
Exté
Helena Sorel
Isabel de Pedro
Lui-Jo
Paula Frani
Roberta Scarpa
Rocco Barocco
Valentino
Versace Jeans Couture

ACCESSORIES
Angela Hale
Rocco Barocco
Versace

SIZES
8–14

RETURNS POLICY
Exchange or credit
note at the manager's
discretion

Verdict
13 Thistle Street
Aberdeen
AB10 1XZ
01224 644 558
Open: Mon – Fri 10 – 5.30
except Thurs 10 – 6.30
Sat 9.30 – 5.30
Sun 12 – 4

Just around the corner from Swanky Modes (see p.202–203) is another *Fashion UK* jewel with an emphasis on grown-up and affluent. Chic, sexy, smart and original, Verdict caters for women of every age. The designers on offer are luxurious rarities, and the quality of service is extremely high.

It's a handsome, even regal-looking shop. Outside, an elaborate tracery of wrought iron climbs around the door and windows, a theme that is continued in the fixtures and fittings inside the shop. A stone-flagged floor, ivory walls and soft furnishings complete the stylized but simple decor. At first, the shop atmosphere may seem a little cool and overly professional, but it quickly becomes clear that the service on offer here is the best of its kind – attentive, friendly but restrained. Free alterations on non-sale goods and previews for regular customers are an added appeal.

Owner Shirley Milne aims to provide exciting looks for women who want to steer clear of hackneyed fashion trends. She dislikes the over-obvious fashion statement. 'The whole idea of Verdict', she says, 'is to provide clothes that women can actually look good in'. Milne is an ex-accountant, and has warmly embraced the greater spontaneity that the fashion world affords. For her, buying is the most pleasurable part of the job. Gifted with a slick eye for detail, she selects clothes instinctively, achieving a good balance between wearability and glamour.

Milne spends a great deal of time on the shop floor as well as in the back office. After four years in the retail business she is more than satisfied with her career change. 'Fashion has always been what I have wanted to do, but I was raised to play it safe. I spent the first part of my life saving money to make this dream a reality and to do it professionally… to do it well.'

ZOOMP

Zoomp
2–6 Jopps Lane
Aberdeen
AB25 1BR
01224 642 152
Open: Mon–Fri 10–5
except Thurs 10–8
Sat 10–6

The decor may be unsophisticated, but the merchandize certainly is not. Zoomp prides itself on carrying a comprehensive range of exclusive cutting-edge designers. From Paul Smith to Chloé, and Philosophy to Lacroix, there's a wide and varied choice of casualwear, daywear and the downright glam. You'll even find the re-emerging Katherine Hamnett, back where she belongs at the forefront of contemporary fashion retail.

The store is located in an obscure street just outside Aberdeen's city centre and on the other side of town to the majority of the city's other independents. The main floor is huge, and there's an equally spacious basement. There is even room at the entrance to leave cumbersome pushchairs and umbrellas.

The atmosphere is welcoming and fun. There's loud party music, and coffee or herbal tea is offered to every customer. Both manager and assistants – all of whom have very individual images of their own – are enthusiastic about the store and its merchandize. Knowledgeable about the products they carry, they offer flexible, engaging shopping advice.

Owner Katia Manson began her retail career in childrenswear, only gradually progressing into womens- and menswear. More recently, however, she has phased out the other two departments in order to fully focus on her ever-expanding womenswear range. Her eye for the sexy and the sophisticated is faultless, making it hard to to leave this shop without making a purchase of some kind. The store also stocks selected designer collections from bygone years, offering fashion trends of past seasons that have managed to stand the test of time.

In the future, Manson promises to continue championing the less predictable names in fashion and also plans to extend the accessory and shoe departments, for complete top-to-toe dressing.

In the Seventies and Eighties when high street multiples chose not to establish in the turbulent city of Belfast, the independent retailers ruled the roost. Service was always a priority in stores that offered a varied choice of clothing under one roof.

Times have long since changed and the city centre is now bursting with retail choice. As a result, very few specialist stores have remained in the heart of the city, instead there has been a proliferation of stores on the Lisburn Road. This busy main arterial, which stretches straight down to Dublin, is within a prosperous location and easy access for consumers within Southern Ireland too.

Now branded the Belfast equivalent to Chelsea's Kings Road, the flourishing Lisburn boutiques, clubs, bars and restaurants are giving Dublin a run for its money, and taking Northern Ireland retailing to new heights.

CARTER CLOTHING

Carter Clothing
11 Upper Queen Street
Belfast
County Antrim
BT1 6LS
02890 243 412
Open: Mon – Sat 9.30 – 5.30
except Thurs 9.30 – 9

Carter Clothing is a traditional Northern Irish independent retailer, created in 1975 and initially specializing in menswear. In 1979 the shop moved to Belfast, and, from the early 1980s, it tentatively took on women's fashion. Owners Dave Pinnick and Andrew Watson had to re-educate themselves to cater successfully to feminine tastes and, realizing that a woman's touch would make all the difference, recruited womenswear buyer Janise Waring.

The store is located in a giant converted building with stone walls and Gothic-looking leaded windows, although the façade has been modernized to create

a clean glass shop front. Inside, the beige carpeting, white walls and expansive shop floor gives Carter a department store feel, though thankfully without the impersonality that would go with it.

Carter Clothing offers couples the chance for some synchronized shopping – on the ground floor, the unisex casual clothing department, with designer jeans and sweats in abundance, leads to men's tailoring, while upstairs the smarter womenswear collection should meet most needs. Staff of all ages appear comfortably stylish, and the level of customer service is high but not overbearing. All twelve of the full-

and part-time assistants are capable of launching into an 'old-style' traditional approach – with two to three hours of attentive service – if required. A happy ending would, of course, entail your ideal purchase of superb quality and fit being wrapped and handed to you with a courteous smile, but free-style browsing is also encouraged.

Carter Clothing has achieved success through directing its service towards a conservative clientele and by sticking to the 'classic with a twist' formula. It is bound to satisfy those looking for a retailer unimpressed by whimsical trends or fly-by-night fashions.

THE GLASSHOUSE

LABELS
L'Altra Moda
Amaya Arzuaga
Amazone
Bernshaw
Custo
Dolce & Gabbana
Homeless
Kenzo
Plein Sud
Versace

ACCESSORIES
Pilgrim
Suzy Smith
Versace

SIZES
10 – 14

REFUND POLICY
Exchange or credit
note for goods returned
within one week

The Glasshouse
3 Bedford House
Bedford Street
Belfast
BT2 7FD
02890 312 964
Open: Mon – Sat 10 – 6

As the name suggests, The Glasshouse sports a genuine glass exterior, allowing passers-by a peek into the interior of this luxuriously furnished store with its unshamedly A-grade designer offerings.

Owner and buyer Donna Mulgrew attributes the shop's success to its constantly changing layout that aims to keep things fresh. Often the latest stock is given the limelight – ideal for regulars craving the latest trends – but at other times Mulgrew will merchandize according to colour or style, adding a wealth of glamorous and exotic accessories to evoke an Aladdin's cave atmosphere. There are three spacious fitting rooms, each kitted out with deep-red walls, comfortable wicker furniture and glass-brick feature. Flanking them is a small lounging area alluringly furnished with a cushion-strewn black-leather sofa.

The model-like staff could prove intimidating to a Glasshouse virgin, but their expert styling skills are certainly a bonus worth taking advantage of. Other appealing Glasshouse customer services include personal shopping, free alterations and the opportunity to order items even before they come into stock. In addition, there's a database that allows listed customers to receive regular updates, invites and discounts.

Glasshouse is the ideal destination for anyone who wants to stay one step ahead of the high-street cavalcade. Mulgrew admits to finding buying in advance of the high street a challenge, but persists in trying to locate the designers that dictate fashion rather than follow it. Head-to-toe must-haves – at the time of writing – include Suzy Smith funky bags, Pilgrim costume jewellery and at least one pair from the exquisite selection of Versace shoes. In The Glasshouse, what you see is what you get – and what you get is gorgeous.

KOKO

Koko
613 Lisburn Road
Belfast
BT9 7GT
02890 687 797
Open: Mon – Sat 9.30 – 5.30

SIZES

6–20

RETURNS POLICY

No refunds. Exchange
or credit note at
manager's discretion

Set up by Sandra and Paul Hamiford, this quality Belfast independant – along with its sister shoe-and-bag shop, Rojo – gives surefire satisfaction to the more mature fashionable shoppers of Northern Ireland. Despite the slightly conventional feel of the shop interior – wooden flooring counterpoised by pastel-blue walls – Koko is a retail force to be reckoned with, offering exclusivity in a relaxed and unpretentious environment.

The life of any store is nurtured by its staff, and in this respect Koko relies heavily on manager Deirdre Delahunt and buyer Michelle Brady. Both women prefer not to use agencies to help them choose stock and are assiduous visitors to the London, Paris and Milan shows. They aim to keep the shop up-to-date without relinquishing their classic roots – and, with them, the more conservative among their Belfast clientele. Diversity and quality of brands – as well as a broad size range – ensure that there is something for everyone here. Classical and avant-garde rub shoulder pads in perfect harmony.

Staff are relaxed and reassuring and clearly enjoy a good rapport with many of their customers. They enjoy giving advice and will go to great lengths to keep their customers – and even their customers' children – happy and satisfied. They keep well abreast of fashion news and trends, so that advice is always authoritative and trustworthy. Assistants are happy to bring in a selection of shoes, bags and other accessories from Koko's twin, Rojo, so that customers can get the complete head-to-toe service. Out-of-hours appointments can be accommodated, but the easy-going atmosphere of the store means that personal consultations can take place happily at any time of the normal working day.

PANACHE

Panache
723 Lisburn Road
Belfast
BT9 7GU
02890 382 796
Open: Mon – Sat 9.30 – 5.30

Panache is set on Belfast's Lisburn Road, the Northern Ireland centre of cutting-edge culture. A busy main road, it's a seemingly incongruous location for a proliferation of designer retailers, clubs, wine bars and restaurants, but it has undoubtedly become a hip and happening new destination for both locals and out-of-towners.

Panache-owner Nina Walls took over the store on its fifth anniversary, and one year on she has a thriving business on her hands. Although she had no previous fashion experience, she has shown flair and tenacity in keeping her finger firmly on the fashion pulse, expanding the company range and image to create an aspirational shopping experience that's characteristic of the BT9 district. While the looks cover the whole spectrum from casual to formal, the ranges Panache carries are limited, sustaining the mood of exclusivity.

The store interior is ultra-modern – both polished and elegant. Its paved and wooden floors, white walls, large mirrors and tastefully recessed lighting give it a gallery-style feel. Three television screens play the latest catwalk collections – an element that adds a distinctive special quality to the shop. The large airy fitting rooms provide ample seating as well as hanging space, along with the thoughtful touch of a robe for changing.

Panache's welcoming atmosphere is also reflected in the groomed, hospitable personae of the women who work there. All the staff are under thirty and degree-educated, and each has her own business card and works with a regular client base. This facet of Panache has enabled the store to establish and build upon an unrivalled staff-customer relationship; staff regularly swap work days to accommodate customer appointments. Such a unique personal touch, together with the staff's intimate familiarity with stock, has created an upmarket environment that nevertheless retains an approachable and accessible character.

The predominant type of shopper at Panache is mature and discerning, yet the store also attracts younger professional women. This latter market is still a growth area for the store, and by carrying brands such as Sportmax – the least expensive of those stocked – it is directly geared towards attracting younger shoppers. When buying new items, Walls has a very clear vision of the needs of her customers. She aims to provide value for money, wearability and exclusivity, and for this reason she sources garments from all over the world. Think individual, think unique.

CHARTY DURRANT SUZANNE
JO ADAMS CHARLES WORTHI
SUZANNE COSTAS FREIWALD
ANYA HINDMARCH WRIGHT &
PROF. HELEN STOREY MATTHE
DR SUSANNAH HANDLEY PET
MATTHEW WILLIAMSON FIOI
CHARLES WORTHINGTON AN
WRIGHT & TEAGUE PETER CO
DR ALISTAIR KNOX CHARTY
PETER COOPER FIONA LANE F
MATTHEW JEATT GEORGINA
DR SUSANNAH HANDLEY LIZ

OSTAS FREIWALD JO ADAMS
TON PETER COOPER LIZ EARL
MATTHEW JEATT FIONA LANE
EAGUE. GEORGINA GOODMAN
WILLIAMSON RUBY HAMMER
COOPER DR ALISTAIR KNOX
LANE GEORGINA GOODMAN
HINDMARCH RUBY HAMMER
ER FUTURE GAZING LIZ EARL
RRANT PROF. HELEN STOREY
BY HAMMER MATTHEW JEATT
ODMAN PROF. HELEN STOREY
RL CHARLES WORTHINGTON

Nothing stays the same in the fashion world, nor should it. That's why this section is devoted to looking at what's happening now in the image industry and, more importantly, what is coming through.

All of the designers and thinkers featured here are at the top of their field. While some experts give a hands-on assessment of where they and we are, others – by nature of their work – approach their theme with a more scientific approach. What does come through, however, is that this book is a pathfinder in its own right. Independent retail culture is credited with providing the service of the future. You have only to observe the approach employed by a department store such as Debenhams to see that creating a designer boutique within a giant depot-style clothing port has gone some way to meeting the demand for a personalized shopping experience. And if the answer to Marks and Spencer's problems proves to be Per Una, it will be because it, too, has contrived a shop within a shop as an antidote to the personality-free warehouse that surrounds it.

Many of the experts here use similar catchwords – intimacy, experience, service, intelligence, unique, original, handcrafted and so on. While all come from very different areas of the fashion industry, their words knit together to plot a clear direction for the next few seasons.

FASHION EDITOR
JO ADAMS

Jo Adams worked as a stylist at the *Independent* for five years before becoming Fashion Editor at the *Observer* in 1996. She has worked freelance for a variety of publications including Australian *Vogue* and British *Marie Claire* and on the BBC television programme *Style Challenge*.

'Clothes can influence the way your day turns out and the way people perceive you, and first impressions count. Clothes give us the opportunity to attract, make a good impression, display status and that's all without considering them as fashion items!

'Trends tend to start at street level and are translated by predictors, designers and then by the fashion media, taking it full circle back to the street. The media certainly influences which trends become more mainstream. Those given less coverage are slower to take off. World events can slowly have an influence. If people are not going out as much and spending more time in, comfort fabrics and relaxed clothing can suddenly become a big statement – "I have nothing to prove; this is my leisure time."

'The length of time a trend lasts depends how it is embraced by the public; hippie is multifaceted and easy to wear. Other trends date very quickly; they look amazing for one season, then as things change they look dated and tired.

'There is always a backlash to huge trends – it could go from unstructured to structured – but I feel the next trend will be stricture and utilitarian dressing.

'High-street labels now seem to have as much respectability as designer clothes. In fact, you are more credibly styled if you find an item from Tesco that people think is Prada. Designers like Luella Bartley are designing with their names up front for New Look, and Top Shop has its own designer label, TS, for which guest designers produce a capsule collection. The focus is on the clever consumer to create a good look. Money no longer equals automatic style. Second-hand and vintage shops are even more fashionable lately as these encapsulate all that fashion is currently about: one-off finds, reasonably priced, yet exclusive. Jigsaw has picked up on this with their vintage line. Sadie Frost even went to the Oscars wearing a vintage Portobello Road dress.

'There is so much choice. Supermarkets are producing successful clothing lines, but are no threat to the high street as they attract a different kind of customer, as do independent stores, stocking designers that are exclusive to them. Here the customer can feel like they are buying something a little more special. A lot of the time the buyers for the store will stock smaller named designers alongside the bigger names, and this makes for a more varied choice and individual wardrobe. Independent stores can also be responsible for influencing designers for high-street stores; they visit smaller boutiques to source ideas. As a fashion editor I can feel intimidated by certain shops. I still don't understand this, but service is the key to a welcoming environment.

'As a nation we enjoy shopping. And all keenly follow trends more than any other European country. Our Italian and French counterparts simply do not enjoy "dressing up" like we Brits.'

Peter Cooper has worked in the textile industry for 33 years. He was the technical executive for Courtaulds Textiles and oversaw the group's environmental affairs worldwide from 1989 to 2001. Since then, he has worked as an independent environmental consultant for a number of well-known clients.

'I do not think that the consumer fully appreciates what is involved in producing clothes in an environmentally friendly way, primarily because the production chain is so long. My role has been to oversee the process and develop and advise where process improvements can be made to achieve greater environmental acceptability. I believe this is the surest way of bringing about improvements in the mass market. The textile chain impacts on the environment in terms of energy use in both production and after-care, in the use of dyes and chemicals to achieve the fashion and performance standards demanded by the consumer, and the waste and packaging produced. However, if we consider the whole process chain for a cotton garment, the environmental impact starts with the herbicides and pesticides used on the farm to ensure a healthy and quality crop.

Wool is also raw material where the balance of a good crop and environmental impact has to be carefully balanced. A great deal has been written about the impact of sheep-dip chemicals, but without pest protection the sheep can be almost eaten alive. Obviously, the best solution would be to develop alternatives that give the animal protection but do not have an impact on the environment.

'The use of synthetic or natural dyes provokes much debate. It is possible to create interesting and exciting colours from natural sources; an example would be obtaining a reddish shade from the remains of the cochineal beetle. However, the amount of beetle residues required to serve the mass market would probably obliterate the beetle population. As a consequence, the use of natural dyes would sustain only a niche market for environmentally improved garments and would probably not reach the wider consumer base.

'I believe garment/clothing and fabric designers should have textile chemistry and/or environmental science as part of their university course. This would ensure that environmentally unsound practices were understood and could be designed out of the process at the start rather than being controlled later, which has been the situation for some time. My view is that the northern Europeans (Germans and Scandinavians) are ahead of the UK in this respect, as environmental affairs appear to be a much more important part of their society. On the other hand, the United States with its current approach to climate change and its objections to the Kyoto Agreements – together with its major influence on the textile and clothing sectors – does not appear to be showing the necessary level of leadership that is required for environmental improvement. Again, my own view is that energy use in production and after-care is the major impact of garments on the environment, and a heightened perception of this is absolutely crucial to the debate and environmental improvement.

'Designers can be very influential. Katharine Hamnett, for example, has investigated the idea of "green cotton" and rethought some of the production methods that were environmentally unfriendly. Unfortunately, she is virtually alone in her efforts to produce garments in this way and production was only on a relatively small scale. To have a real effect, the fundamental changes have to take place on a wider scale and at the beginning of the process.

'The positive changes that have taken place over the past few years have been: the development of organic cotton and ranges of wool goods made from recycled material; the publication of environmental requirements for suppliers by a number of high-street chains, leading to such improvements as the reduction of the impact of chromium in some dyes; and the development of "eco-labels" (once again, a bigger trend in northern Europe than in the UK). There has also been legislation on packaging recovery and recycling and a movement to reuse and recycle energy and utilities. There is still some way to go on this one, however.

'Future changes are very much dependent on a public and political desire to be proactive. The consumer must want to spend on environmentally improved garments to create a market and to produce a reward (i.e. profit) for the store and the supplier. The industry, too, needs to be more proactive about the benefits of environmental improvement. The cost benefits and competitive advantage of environmentally friendly production need to be accepted as possibilities. And of course Western governments need to have the environment higher on their political agenda, as it was in the early Nineties.'

DENIM DESIGNER
SUZANNE COSTAS FREIWALD

Earl Jean was launched in 1996 by LA-based Suzanne Costas Freiwald – a former television and film stylist. Her personally tailored vintage denims were such a hit with friends that she began designing full-time and now sells in America, Europe and Japan.

'Denim fabric has not been affected so much by new technology but by a return to the old methods of manufacturing it. There is also a return to past materials, such as real indigo combined with an old-fashioned ammonia finish. This gives denim a cool, flat, hand-finished effect.

'There has been a technological revolution in denim-finishing though, which produces an authentic-looking faded, worn jean. Resins, enzymes, hand-sanding, oven-baking, bleach sprays, and advances in stonewashing, have produced amazing results.

'This new technology had barely begun in the mid-Nineties when Earl started; the only artificially faded jean on the market was a stonewash that looked really fake. Rather than wear this look, people would buy dark jeans and let them fade naturally – it was the only way at that time to achieve cool faded jeans. Earl's first jeans were dark denim; it was a desire for the simple – the authentic.

'Another recent change is, of course, the addition of stretch. Today's stretch denim actually looks like real denim – not that spongy stretch denim we saw in the 1980s. The current stretch comes with all the attributes of good denim…and we are able to achieve great washes…Also, stretch is more production-friendly than it used to be; shrinkage is more controlled and dependable, so good fit can be

attained. The improvement of stretch denim over the past five years has coincided nicely with the evolution of our denim products. While, I am a believer in very classic traditional old-school denim, a great authentic-looking jean in a comfortable stretch is a good thing.

'Our first jean, Style 55, was the first of it's kind on the market – a slim, long, dark-denim, low-rise jean, with a slight boot-cut, modest labelling, and minimal to no advertising. Variations of the 55 are still our best-sellers. Trend-wise, Earl is now into higher rises, twisted side seams, and unusual blown-out colours.

'I think that the low slim jean with a good-looking wash will be around for quite a while. There will be small trends within this larger one that will come and go, like ultra low-rise, embellished jeans, exaggerated whiskers or sandblasting. I am not interested in hitting one of these little trend pockets. I'm more inspired by a brand that is high end – think Wrangler for Harvey Nichols or Barneys.

'I'm sure women will be wearing their jeans with £500 heels and an YSL top at night or with flip-flops and a vintage T-shirt during the day for some time yet. Denim has been a must-have, for women for a long time – almost a uniform classic that changes with time. If you look at old photos of Woodstock, an Aerosmith concert, a night at Studio 54, or an episode of *Charlie's Angels*, everyone is wearing denim. We forget because during the 1980s, women's denim looked pretty bad so the fashion set took a break. Today jeans are the new cool thing and a must-have in a woman's wardrobe.'

For more details of Suzanne's work, go to www.earljean.com.

CHARTY DURRANT

STYLIST

Charty Durrant has worked for a variety of publications including *Vogue* and the *Sunday Times*. As a freelancer, she is employed in commercial and editorial fields and works for supermodels and pop stars as a personal stylist.

'A woman shouldn't look styled. It should look effortless. Over-prepared is a real turn-off for me. These days everyone is bombarded with imagery of what the look is. I don't subscribe to the "Get the look" approach pioneered by *Vogue*. I prefer "Get your own look" one that celebrates your individuality. Keep hold of who you are and build your own visual identity with clothes.

'We're flooded with choice, and women need individuality. The motivation behind the current preoccupation for vintage is understandable. It is practically a one-off. You know you aren't going to see someone in the same thing. Choosing clothes is about what resonates. It's okay to be emotive about a choice rather than feel that your choices should be dictated by images in magazines. That comes with confidence. Knowing yourself and your body is crucial, but also approaching the season with a basic knowledge is helpful, too. Extreme styles that are much photographed tend to have a shelf life, whereas quieter pieces can have more longevity. Those are the pieces that could become personal vintage.'

Liz Earle is an award-winning author of more than thirty books and the creator of the Naturally Active Skincare product range. She regularly appears on television and is an active campaigner, co-founding the Guild of Health Writers and FLAG – the Food Labelling Agenda. She is also patron of the National Eczema Society.

'I originally developed the Naturally Active Skincare range for my own sensitive skin and started out with three golden rules. First and foremost the products had to work. Years spent researching my beauty and health books convinced me herbs and vitamins are the gentle, yet powerful, key to great-looking skin. Secondly, the daily routine had to be simple, with no-fuss products. Each product is designed to work hard, often in two or three different ways, to maximise time and minimise effort. Last, but not least, I also believe think we all want something special, a pampering bit of luxury (hence we use fabulously scented essential oils).

'We're primarily a mail-order company because this is the way ahead. Our genuine motto at Liz Earle By Mail from day one has always been "quality and service always". I think that if you apply that to everything you do in life then you can't go far wrong. The future is all about giving exceptional service.

'New ingredients hold some of the most excitement for the future. Skincare is polarising into two camps – high-tech or natural. I favour the more natural approach, as I believe it has more to offer in the long term. We don't use ingredients such as AHAs (one of the more recent buzzwords in cosmetic chemistry), as these fruit acids are known to trigger skin sensitivity in some. Likewise, we don't use any chemical sunscreens, as they can sensitise the skin and may even accelerate skin ageing by encouraging free radical activity. Instead, we use mineral sunscreens, high levels of antioxidant vitamins such as natural vitamin E (from plant oils) to help delay the signs of ageing – both proven to be more natural and more effective. So many botanical extracts have stood the test of time, such as camomile as an anti-inflammatory, aloe vera to soften and the herb echinacea to encourage stronger skin. We now have a company botanist, and we're looking at plant extracts that foam for a detergent-free shower gel. Many skincare benefits already exist in nature.

'The beauty industry is largely built on dreams, but there's no such thing as an instant quick fix. Botox injections may erase a wrinkle, but they could also paralyse your face! The best way to get good-looking skin is with gentle, daily, high-quality natural ingredients. It's best to coax the skin into behaving well, not bully it with shock tactics. The long-term results are better. Also remember that most beauty models are still in their teens and have the benefit of great make-up, lighting and air-brushing to remove every blemish – not very realistic when an advert might be aimed at a women in her fifties. I'm more concerned about skin comfort and encouraging glowing good health, not scrutinising every line. Life is too precious to get hung up on wrinkles – they just mean you've had happy times and laughed a lot, which is a good thing.'

For more details of Liz Earle's work, go to www.lizearle.com.

SHOE DESIGNER
GEORGINA GOODMAN

Georgina Goodman began life as a fashion assistant on *i-D* magazine and later pursued the dream of becoming a shoe designer. Having graduated from the Royal College of Art she is shortly to open a couture shoe shop in Mayfair and is Manolo Blahnik's hot tip.

'A girl needs two things in life – a good hairdresser and a good cobbler. Shoes are friends and deserve good care; in fact when you listen to women talking about shoes, they use language charged with emotion. I never hear anyone talking about an item of clothing in the same way. Women have an emotional and sexual attachment to shoes. A great pair of shoes can engender pure lust. Then there is the love affair with the shoe that delivers glamour and comfort in one go. The classic heel will never diminish in women's affections, but height is less of a priority. Originally we were attracted to shoes that reduced the size of our feet, the pointy stiletto and heel did the job. It was the Cinderella complex. Women enjoy the extra length at the front of the shoe and the lower heel of recent seasons; we're no longer preoccupied with dainty feet.

'We've had an interesting few years in shoe design. The industry, originally a slow and lumbering business worrying about the phenomenal rise of the trainer, has revived its influence. Shoes and accessories for the big design houses are where the profit is. The price and the sizing is much more inclusive than an item of clothing, so designer shoes have almost become mass-produced.

'Those looking for something new, have returned to hand-crafted effect or finish; although the shoes may have still been largely put together by machine, the appearance of a crafted shoe, with visible stitching and leather uppers and soles, has dominated the designer footwear market. The hand-crafted finish, with a more classic shape, has really taken over from the ultra-modern styles.

'I have been working in the bespoke area, and it's authenticity that I seek to create. For example, a cowboy boot is authentic. It's been made with traditional methods and speaks a language unaltered by seasonal trends. I believe we are in a transitional phase at the moment, and that the higher end of shoe design will take on a personalised bespoke energy. In the future, consumers who have the money will want their shoes to be authentic and retain value regardless of catwalk whims.

'All designers have a responsibility to think about what they are creating. The product that they send into the world needs to be relevant for a lot longer than a seasonal trend. In a mass-produced society it's hard to think in those terms. But I love the idea that my shoes will have value and meaning and may be passed from mother to daughter or on to a museum. I see myself as a facilitator of dreams. It won't necessarily make me rich, but it will make me happy.'

For more details of Georgina's work, go to www.georginagoodman.com

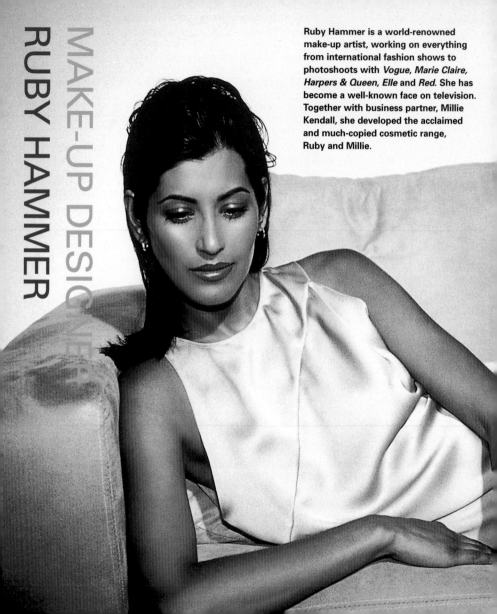

MAKE-UP DESIGNER
RUBY HAMMER

Ruby Hammer is a world-renowned make-up artist, working on everything from international fashion shows to photoshoots with *Vogue, Marie Claire, Harpers & Queen, Elle* and *Red*. She has become a well-known face on television. Together with business partner, Millie Kendall, she developed the acclaimed and much-copied cosmetic range, Ruby and Millie.

'A few seasons ago, it was all bare and shiny skin. There was a period where one item of make-up was asked to perform a variety of tasks. We're not streamlining in that way any more, and now that women are using more make-up, minimalist make-up bags have gone out the window.

'Glamour and quality are current watchwords in the make-up industry. Fashionable colours are less of a priority than the texture and feel of a product. There are fewer rules about what you wear and how you wear it; models may be coming down the catwalk with heavily painted faces, but that's just theatre.

'There is much more information, so consumers are more discerning and that breeds confidence. There is less worry about being "in fashion". Make-up is all things to all women; it allows you to hide behind it and has the power to act as a mask. There are days when I like to experiment. And there are days when I like to mask or change something about myself. Ultimately, make-up should be a resource. I don't think women feel that they should be wearing it all the time any more. Barefaced and bare-skinned is a much more regular occurrence.

'The biggest changes that have taken place in recent years are to do with the quality and feel of product on the skin. Developments include make-up with light-reflective particles, skin treatments that are part of the make-up, and choice of finish: matt, shine, shimmer, glowing… Texture in make-up right now is huge.

'The Ruby and Millie make-up range was started in 1998. I didn't feel there had been anything big in make-up since Mary Quant, and we wanted to make an impact. Our aim was unique packaging and good formulation combined with accessibility. The packaging has been so thoroughly copied that we need to evolve ours further. It's an acknowledgement that we are innovators, and we take the copying in that vein.

'Key make-up items I advise are eyelash curlers – they are beautifully made these days and are no longer items of torture – Q-tips and lipbalm. Concealer is a woman over thirty's best friend. Skin starts to change after your twenties, and then it's not enough to simply apply a base of foundation to cover the face, you have to use concealer skillfully to even out the skin tones. Invest in a good set of brushes – the general rule is powder products need brushes.

'Future developments will be seen with foundations. Airbrushing techniques – at the moment only available at a price to celebrities – will be delivered to a mainstream audience. Beautiful skin is the thing we all strive to present, and cosmetics are reaping the benefits of developments in skincare. The goal will be to deliver the most high-tech benefits such as airbrushed make-up in an affordable way. There are some big companies investing in that. We're developing a new foundation, which is completely differently packaged. The components alone have taken a long time to research.

'There will be more East-West exchange. The Japanese market is streets ahead, and I think more western countries will incorporate eastern approaches to skincare (for instance, little girls there are taught to value their skin from an early age and to understand the importance of diet, massage and moisturiser).'

DR SUSANNAH HANDLEY

FABRIC & TEXTILES ACADEMIC

Dr Susannah Handley has appeared on television and radio and has written for _GQ_, _Blue Print_ and _The Herald Tribune_, amongst others. She has curated exhibitions for a variety of museums, including the V&A, and is Senior Tutor for Research at the Royal College of Art's School of Fashion & Textiles.

'Design is driven by cultural and lifestyle change, and the most dramatic innovation to impact on all our lives is the ubiquitous computer chip. Technologically enhanced fabrics and hybrid products are the Holy Grail for future manufacturers, and this quest has brought about a meeting of aliens – weavers, engineers and chemists. Many large corporate companies such as Motorola, Philips, Levi Strauss, Adidas, France Telecom and even Courrèges are in a research race to prototype the products of the future. It is an exciting time for everyone, a design adventure – a kind of fashion/science sans frontières.

'As any good designer will tell you, the cloth, and the way it behaves, is the crucial element in creating a silhouette. More and more risks are being taken with materials that were never intended for or used before in fashion. We just have to think of Hussein Chayalan to realize the impact of switching material contexts.

'The marriage of fashion and science seems a strange coupling but when it works, it works extremely well. One recent example of this is the invention of a spray-on fabric (cotton in a can) by Manel Torres. Here we have a fashion designer who had a dream and with the help of some chemical expertise made it come true. Out of an aerosol can we can make an instant T-shirt, pocket or embroidery.

'A new species of multifunctional, almost "living" garment is beginning to invade fashion's territory, engineered by scientists and technologists and created from "interactive" and "responsive" materials. These hyperactive materials can monitor our physical condition, calm our stress levels and respond to climate extremes and environmental pollution.

'We have already seen mainstream fashion collections made from bullet-proof, fireproof and knife-retardant fabrics and clothes with built-in light and sound effects. On the drawing board, if not the cutting table, we can anticipate clothing that can identify and memorize the different objects you carry with you and clothes that will remind you to take your keys and wallet with you when leaving home or that can warn you when your pocket is being picked.

'The fashion industry functions in a fairly antiquated way, and the signs are that unless it changes in a fairly radical way, it will miss the greatest opportunities for innovation since the invention of synthetic materials. Imagine a textile with the ability to change shape, colour and texture, just like a living organism – well, it might become the next reality.

'We live in a world of increasingly blurred boundaries, where biology, nano-technology, electronics and textiles meet not only in the wardrobe but also in the home. Fabrics clothe our walls, floors, furniture and bedding. Here, too, we will see the softening of technology. Wouldn't it be better to wake up to a "Digital Dawn" where your electro-luminescent (fine-silk and couched-embroidered) pillow and duvet gradually light up – much better than a shrill alarm call.'

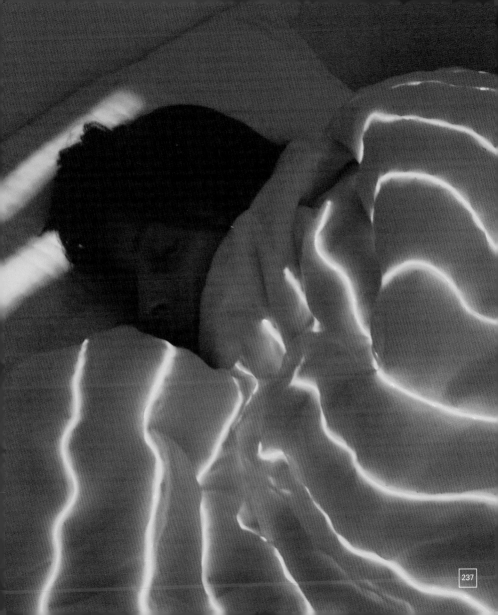
237 of 276

237

Anya Hindmarch began trading in 1988 aged nineteen and has since won British Accessory Designer of the Year many times. Selling all over the world from her own stores and with concessions in international department stores she offers mainline and Blue Label collections as well as her own leather-goods range.

'The accessories market has grown because bags and all the other extras are a quick way to update any outfit. A bag is also such an easy purchase to make. There are no sizing issues and you don't have to spend time trying them on.

'Women express themselves through their accessories and rather than being safe are now happy wearing sequinned, embroidered, patchwork, "graphitized" bags and beyond. I think women view their handbag as a big reflection of their style. But a bag is more than an item of clothing; it has an emotional currency, it is what we use to carry our lives around.

'There has been a big shift in the bag market, towards lesser-known makes, with many companies being daring with colour and shape. Trends featuring fringing have tied in with the whole peasant look that has been so popular. The next big trend will be big soft bags with the emphasis still on casual chic but using luxurious fabrics like ponyskin, butter-soft nappa leather and so on.

'On top of the clothing trends, there is also a "trend bag" each season – often dictated by the main designers. Look at the Dior saddlebag, the Prada bowling bag and the Fendi baguette. A big reason for this is the advertising machine behind the label, which gets the bags get a lot of coverage, making them very covetable as the next fashion must-have. People generally wear these bags to death because the style is associated with a certain period and can seem a bit "last season", once the moment has passed'.

'People recognize our bags by the logo, which is a little bow. Signature bags vary from our fun Blue Label print bags with kitsch images of animals and old photographs to our classic leather day bags. We now do such a variety of accessories that it's hard to pin down one signature item. Our "Be a Bag" project has been hugely successful. We launched it by asking style icons and celebrities to donate personal photographs, which we then incorporated in panels on the bag. These were sold for charity, but it was a fantastic way to launch the business.

'The best way of confirming whether a bag is well made is to look at the inside of the bag. A good-quality lining is the best indication of a well-constructed bag.'

For more details of Anya's work, go to www.anyahindmarch.com

PREDICTION CONSULTANT
MATTHEW JEATT

Matthew Jeatt has been called many things: trend tracker, relativist and corporate relationship counsellor. After fifteen years in the music industry and ten years at Promostyl UK, he retains a keen interest in cultural development and its influence upon fashion.

'The emerging shopping culture values individuality, elegance and quality. This is a direct reaction to the uniform, casual, global style predominant over the last ten to fifteen years.

'Fashion does not exist in a vacuum and, until recently, has simply reflected the trend towards globalization. The best example is probably the trend towards an urban uniform (combat-pant variants, jeans-style jackets, urban colours: stone, concrete, greys, metallics and baseball caps), which is a style you will find in all major cities of the world from New York to London to Moscow. This suited the brands and manufacturers in the Eighties and Nineties as they could make one product and sell it internationally.

'Today fashion reflects a different trend, one that rejects the global in favour of the local. Local in this regard does not only mean regional, but also refers to the individual's imaginative skills, as opposed to the corporate vision of the world. The work of individual designers is highly valued as we wonder at their imagination, their creativity, and their sense of humour. The skills of artisans and craftspeople are similarly valued. Galliano, Castelbajac, Balenciaga are expressive and at times extreme. Stella McCartney is valued less for her individual expression and more for her ability to design for herself and her friends (another version of local).

'The fashion industry used to create garments two years to eighteen months ahead of season in order to have their products in store at the right time. Now, businesses (Zara, Per Una) demand a quicker response to trend and sales data, and require short-ordering and no-minimum-order quantities.

Consequently, designs can progress from concept to store in ten or twelve weeks.

'Fashion used to be a dictator telling consumers what to wear. The whole industry has turned on its head, and fashion now reflects the needs and desires of the consumer. Couture looks to the street for inspiration, and it is this unique ability that UK-trained designers have that has led them take over couture. (Look at McQueen's image versus YSL's.)

'Shops and businesses that offer the "uniform" model, such as Gap, have struggled to remain relevant. Today people are attracted to small, individual, eclectic shops and have returned to an older model of retailing – the boutique.

'A boutique is a store that reflects an individual focus. You feel connected to the shop-owner and their tastes in a way that is impossible when shopping at a department store. The products change as the interests of the shop owner change. These stores are alive in a very human way and offer a great contrast to shopping at brand temples where you are asked to conform to brand values and a one-product-many-consumers range.

'Shops of the future will have to more accurately reflect our needs and desires. Styles will have to become ergonomic and reflect the real and infinitely variable nature of our bodies rather than the model size 8. Shops will have to become places that we enjoy visiting and that will welcome us even when we do not buy. This is where shop staff – relevant to their customers (same age, similar interests, specialist knowledge) – will morph from salesperson into friend giving us honest advice. It is this that will have us returning time and time again.'

SIZING EXPERT

DR ALISTAIR KNOX

Dr Alistair Knox heads the Size-Shape-Fit research unit at Nottingham Trent University, which has established a worldwide reputation. Researchers have scanned nearly 11,000 adults on behalf of a consortium of UK retailers.

'Ever since the sewing machine enabled the mass-production of ready-to-wear clothing, the question of 'best average' sizes for garments has been an issue. The need for a simple list of stock options, originally driven by military uniform requirements and now by fashion retailers, is at odds with the infinite variations in human shape.

'This sizing system is fifty years old, so new research is important. People have generally got bigger in recent decades, as a result of better health, diet, and lifestyle changes. People do not fall into neat sets of size measurements; all those with a particular girth or height do not have the same bust size or leg length.

'One of the biggest problems is that the interpretation of size and fit is at the discretion of each manufacturer and retailer and can even vary between styles. Also, size labelling can be abused for marketing purposes as this affects consumer buying decisions. Finally, size labelling is non-standard. The widely used 10-12-14-16 scales in the UK, North America and Australia are all slightly different. Even European metric systems come in a multitude of guises in different countries. A size 12 in the UK is 44 in Italy, 38 in Germany, 40 in Belgium and France.

'Today's average dress size is 14/16 compared to 12/14 fifty years ago. Even the definition of a size 14 has evolved; a woman's waist is thicker in comparison.

Some companies have already amended some of their size charts and block patterns to reflect research results.

'The SizeUK project carried out in 2001/02 with support from the DTI was done in conjunction with sixteen major UK fashion companies and eight academic institutions. This involved scanning with the latest 3-D whole-body scanner, combined with some manual measurements, such as weight, and market-research data. Results will give the largest-ever set of data on body size and shape for the UK's adult population. It is expected that not only traditional measurements statistics will be updated, but also new insights into 3-D-shape analysis will lead to better average fit for ready-made garments.

'The future offers some interesting opportunities: 3-D-scanned body data can be used with standard computer grading and pattern-cutting systems to create bespoke patterns to fit the individual. Presently this is limited to simple garment types or to particular prototype situations, but it is expected to develop further and be more widely applicable.

'3-D scanners and associated software systems will become more advanced and widespread. Personal data including body profile will be storable on a smart card. This will allow size and shape information to be exchanged with computer-aided pattern design and Unit Production System garment assembly. There will still be a cost premium for made-to-measure clothing, but it will be a more realistic twenty to thirty per cent extra. This will open up this market and provide a lifeline for small, local manufacturers who embrace the new technology.'

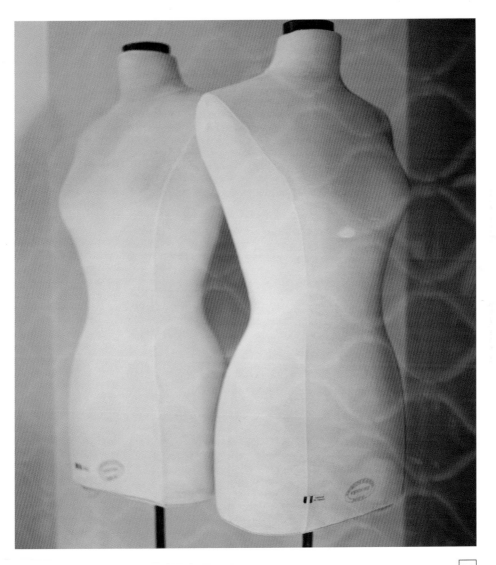

EYEWEAR DESIGNER
FIONA LANE

Fiona Lane is a founder of Fabris Lane, the anglo-italian eyewear company that produces Fabris Lane, Fabris Lane Sport and Mondo UK. The company also collaborates with established designers to develop their own collections.

'The biggest trend to hit the market recently has been coloured lenses. Over the past few seasons the tinting and finishes have become extremely sophisticated. Colour is everywhere, but it's much more subtle and wearable than before. And it's the finish on the lens that gives the polished look. We tint our lenses by using two tones of colour, which are then subtly graduated together from dark to light. We then apply a very fine layer of metal on the part of the lens, which gives a mirror effect. Sunglasses are now viewed almost like jewellery.

Having a wardrobe of sunglasses allows for the wearer to experiment with different identities; there can be the stark classic look or the colourful girlie styles, and some tinted lenses are even restful or playful, enhancing the mood of the wearer in a positive way. We've homed in on subtlety. The oyster colours we've created are so pale that it's like almost wearing a shimmering make-up. Women look immediately good and feel good with little effort. Glasses can make a woman feel dressed.

'We're always looking to find the best base materials to improve quality and protection. There is a handcrafted element to what we do, and our Fabris Lane range is made in Italy and finished by hand. Playing around with colour and working with good lens manufacturers is a big part of the ongoing development where our fashion frames are concerned. We try to choose as early as we can the colours that are important to our collection, in time for the technical team to come back to us with tones of colours. We are also experimenting with coatings. This is where fashion meets technology.

'There was a trend for barely-there frames started by Chanel and Prada. It's a great way of inconspicuously wearing colour. Sunglasses are a perfect way of changing your look without spending a lot of money. All the focus goes to the face. We have classic understated tortoiseshell for when you don't want to make a big statement and then there are the coloured lenses, which can affect your outlook. The colour through which you see the world can have a big effect on your day.

'Things have changed radically now that celebrities are happy to be photographed in their frames. I think the quality of designer frames has extended the remit of eyewear. Designers have realized the profit that can be generated by accessories and so are all creating their own eyewear collections. Having seen them photographed on top models and pop stars, our perceptions of what it is to wear glasses has changed. Prada and Helmut Lang are so good at taking a classic and giving it a new modernity – their frames have been very influential.

'Looking ahead, colour, and sophisticated application of colour, is it is the way forward. Clean lines are still important, but as a foil against these barely-there styles I think plastic will emerge as a stronger element in frames.

'To choose a pair of glasses, face the mirror and try on frame after frame; if you want a look – square frames, for instance – you'll find enough variety to pick a style. I don't subscribe to the school of thought that dictates certain frames for specific face shapes. Although in general, it's best not to mirror your face shape too much.'

For more details of Fiona Lane's work, go to www.fabrislane.com

THEORIST
PROF. HELEN STOREY

Helen Storey ran her own fashion label from 1984 to 1995. During this time she was awarded Most Innovative Designer and Best Exporter and nominated for British Designer of the Year twice in succession. Now a theorist, professor and writer, Storey's recent projects include the ground-breaking Primitive Streak and MENTAL exhibitions, which have toured internationally.

'Most women want fashion to be a part of how they project who they are – an unspoken but crucial communication tool that signals to the outside world how they wish to be viewed.

'As women age, however, the strength and development of their minds becomes as important – for some, more important – and a woman will create (consciously or unconsciously) a uniform that is in effect the essence of "her" and which needs very little changing wherever she goes. Fashion has less and less of an influence as women mature, and one could say that it is an industry that makes the most money out of those who are still defining themselves.

'I think fashion is intrinsically woven into our lives. In this country the ability of our young designers to create it in the image of, and as a response to, the world around them is spectacular. But more importantly, fashion offers a visual language that interacts in a significant way with the growing-up process, where girls travel towards becoming women and, to a lesser but still notable degree, boys struggle to become men.

'Despite this, fashion is not as culturally rated as it should be. Often it is taken for granted, and as the creations of many of our most famous designers fall somewhere between an art and a trade, so the support that might be given at manufacturing and governmental level is at best hit and miss.

'Broadly, I work and create projects that dance across art, science, technology, design and fashion and textiles. My last two projects entitled 'Primitive Streak' (the first 1,000 hours of life seen through textiles and dress) and 'MENTAL' (the visualisation of five creative states of mind) travelled all around the world and were seen collectively by over 2.5 million people. I relish the idea that I can communicate with people's minds, not just their bodies, and that an idea has time to be developed and thoroughly researched; the six-month seasons of the fashion industry didn't suit me!

'When I was a conventional fashion designer, my clothes were loaded with messages and meaning, often at odds with the needs of the commercial collection. I have always used fashion, especially in my early career, to exorcise angry, young, ambitious self-determining ideas – hence the bullets, clothes shredded to an inch of their lives and the glamorisation of the second-hand. Not all designers do this, and it is perhaps because I couldn't get all the meaning I needed to express through fashion alone that I sought the design challenges of working with other industries too.

'Clothes are undeniably full of meaning, from the minute you part with your money for them to how you take care of them, to who you choose to wear them with, to how long you keep them and what experiences they let you recall. Clothes are tangible memory.'

MATTHEW WILLIAMSON

LIFESTYLE DESIGNER

After graduating from Central Saint Martin's in 1994 Matthew Williamson received unprecedented press interest for a small capsule collection modelled by a host of supermodels. His colourful and decorative designs are his signature, and in October 2001 he expanded to create Matthew Williamson Home.

'It's hard to say what's in the future for clothes. I think, generally, designers are tending to stick to what they know best. Rather than one big trend, it seems that there are more options available to us now, as designers focus on what they have become known for. I constantly strive to push my brand values and signature style rather than following a trend. What I do is interesting colour combinations, and feminine, sexy clothes that women feel special in. I love the fusion of East meets West and find constant inspiration in places like Bali and Thailand. I never run short of ideas – if anything, I have too many and often have to edit down. It is important to move on in terms of shape, silhouette and so on, but is also important to have a consistency in your work, so the customer can understand what your label is about. Getting the balance right is a challenge.

'Now that the boho trend has been well and truly covered from designers to the high street, it will only be a matter of time before we see a shift towards more formal, glamorous styles. Fashion is such a cyclical thing and before long we'll all be reacting against the current prevalent trend. I also think designers will continue to focus on what they consider to be their trademarks, and we should see a broader spectrum of options as a result.

'The creative process of designing has to work in harmony with the need to build a business, and each designer has a very different take on this one – my personal challenge is to create a perfect balance between the creative and the business aspects of my job. I think this is what's most exciting about being a designer. It's one thing being creative, but it's turning your ideas into desirable products that people want to own that's the real test.

'Very few people are creative and business-minded at the same time. Luckily for me, I love both aspects. I also have an excellent business partner, Joseph Velosa, who has been with me since the start of my business. If you are a fashion designer with no business skills and you want to run a business, you need to find someone who has those skills. Designing is the easy, fun bit, but that's only about ten per cent of the bigger picture, and lots of new designers overlook this aspect.

'Understanding what customers want at any given time is also a challenge. I try to inform myself wherever possible as to what women want. This is invaluable if you want to improve what you do. I don't know what it's like to wear the clothes so I'm constantly canvassing the opinions of the women who do. But any designer's biggest challenge is having the money to fund and expand business in a way that feels right. I've been branching out into other product areas, so that I can create a lifestyle approach to my work. In this country it's difficult enough to survive, let alone expand. We tend not to take fashion as seriously as other fashion capitals, and that's a great shame.

'My move into home and gifts is based on a simple desire to offer a small piece of the Matthew Williamson brand at an affordable price. I love interior design and the candle range seemed an obvious thing to do. I'm currently developing a larger range of bath, body and home products, as the reaction to them has been fantastic. That has a lot to do with retailers' support. The people who sell our products are a crucial part of the process. We try to keep in touch with all our stockists and keep them informed of any developments within the business. If you don't have a shop of your own, it's vital that your stockists understand who you are and what your label is about. I rely on them to show my collection in the best possible light. A good retailer will always have a good relationship with the designer. Within the shop there will be a good buyer and visual merchandiser and great sales staff who understand the clothes.

'On the whole, British designers have only just begun to focus on expansion through lifestyle products. A lot of talent tends to be picked up by international houses. I think this trend will continue as we are widely considered to be the most creative city. For my part, I would like to continue pushing the work I do. I work approximately six months in advance. As soon as one collection is over, I'm straight on to the next one. It takes this long to do research, design, order fabrics, pattern-cut and produce. I'm enjoying showing in New York, and I am also putting more work into developing the home and body range. But most importantly, I try to take each day as it comes and enjoy what I do.'

For more about Matthew's work, go to www.matthewwilliamson.co.uk

HAIRDRESSER

CHARLES WORTHINGTON

Charles Worthington is twice winner of British Hairdresser of the Year and has five salons in London, tending to more than 2,000 clients each week. He also has award-winning product lines selling in ten countries.

'Experience is the new currency nowadays. Having your hair cut is a necessity, but it should feel like the ultimate luxury. People work long hours, and in their free time they want to experience as much pleasure as possible. A good salon can transform the business of going for a trim or a cut into a wonderful sensual time with head massages, perfumed candles, gentle ambient music, in serene surroundings, with a choice of beauty treatments and a carefully thought-out menu of food and drinks. A holistic approach to hair that involves the whole body is the way forward. I'm often told I'm a gentle hairdresser – which doesn't mean that I don't do edgy or graphic styles – but I do believe in touching a person gently and respectfully. I want clients to leave any of my salons feeling as though they've been treated to first-class service.

'The future for hair is all about health. Hair is now so much sleeker. Shine is crucial because it signifies vitality. In the past people just wanted curl and volume at any cost. They fried, burnt and dried out their hair, and the shine was often non-existent as a result. The reason clients demand silky, shiny glossy hair is because it paints a picture of health and effortless sophistication. Society is much more health-conscious. We care about what we eat and how our skin is ageing. If your hair is glossy and shiny you look groomed and in control of your life.

'So much has changed in the last few years...the tools in the salon as well as the styling products have developed and because of the culture of celebrity magazines, people are often inspired to have something different when they come into the salon. This has helped hairdressers to be more creative...we're all working towards a common goal of making each client look and feel fantastic.

'Listening is a real skill, and not all hairdressers are good at it. Good salons offer free consultation, and a stylist who has listened properly will give you feedback and help you feel confident about the haircut you are about to have.

'I'm currently cutting hair when it is dry. We still wash the hair, condition it and dry it, but with this technique the client and I can see the shape evolving and get an excellent idea of how it's really going to look when it's finished. I can create two hairstyles in one by drying curly hair straight and then cutting into a directional look, then when it is washed and returned to curly, it's completely different.

'The products I have developed in the last few years have all been about demystifying the process of looking good and giving our clients the help they need. I want whatever lotion I'm producing to do the bulk of the work so that the actual expertise of the user is enhanced.

'We have a vision that is about sensuality and serenity and that's why we've extended our reach beyond hair. It stands to reason that someone who is using sophisticated products on their hair will want to use them on their body, too. I learned about skin in order to utilise skincare ingredients in a haircare range. That's why our Outer Body range was such a natural progression. Ultimately, I want to be able to deliver consistent first-class service either in person or through my products.'

For more about Charles Worthington, go to www.charlesworthington.co.uk

JEWELLERY DESIGNERS

WRIGHT & TEAGUE

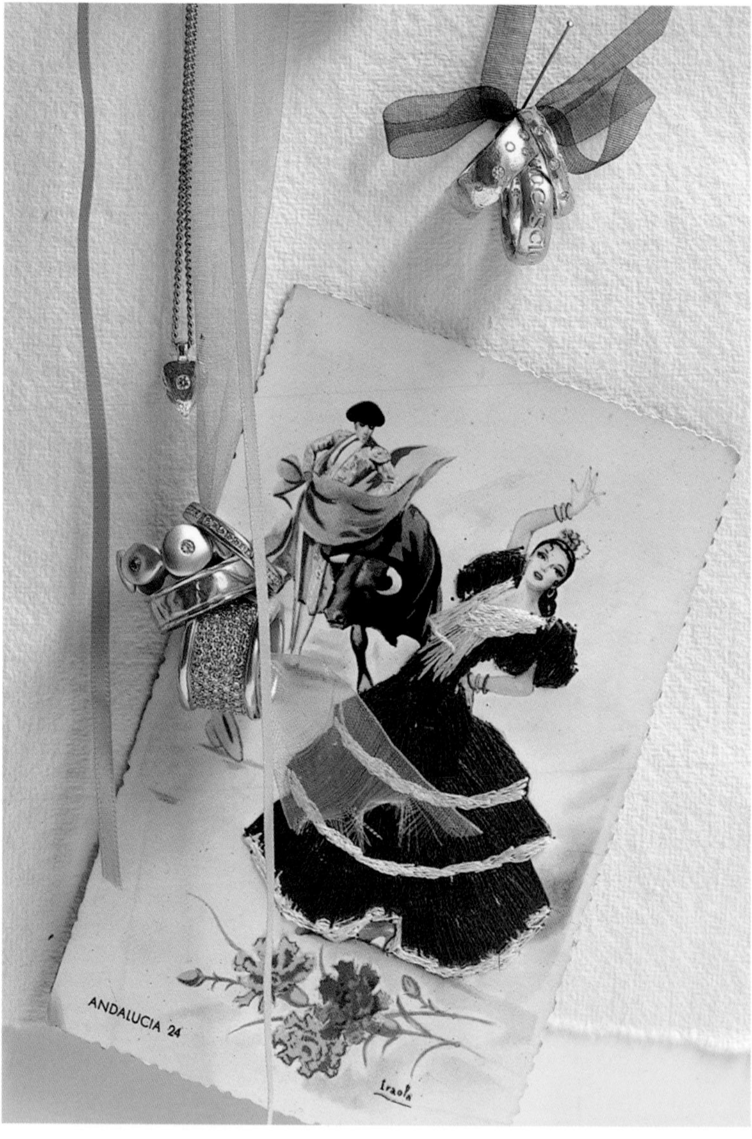

Gary Wright and Sheila Teague began designing as Wright and Teague in 1984, and opened their shop in Mayfair in 1998.

'All people throughout history, not just women, have a relationship with jewellery that fulfils basic primitive needs, including adornment, self-expression, status, fashion and so on. The giving and receiving of jewellery by loved ones is a highly personal act, which may commemorate a special event (wedding, birthday, anniversary) or experience. Subsequently regarded as a love token, or lucky charm, the jewellery acquires an emotional value, a talismanic quality that transcends monetary value.

'Recent seasons have featured a proliferation of hippie chic and folkloric clothing statements that beg for ethnic and tribal jewellery, featuring turquoise, coral, feathers, shells and so on. It is an integral part of the look. Other seasons might be more minimal, perhaps with little emphasis on accessories of any kind. Jewellery however does not need to wait for a fashion stylist. It is the original styling aid – man wore beads before clothes!

'Trends-wise, pieces that reflect the current bohemian mood include anything textural and hand-beaten (having the integrity of time-worn ancient relics), plus turquoise, coral, bone, wood, leather and feathers. Charm bracelets continue to be very strong and men's and children's jewellery are receiving more attention. Our carefully sourced tribal jewellery and vintage pieces are chosen to reflect the Wright & Teague design sensibility, and perfectly complement the eclecticism of what is currently happening in fashion.

'Jewellery trends are governed by what the clothing designers do (the Prairie look giving us Navajo-style jewellery; Victoriana suggesting jet and so on). But there are jewellery trends in their own right. Celebrities like Kylie and David Beckham have definitely been influential, and major world political events like September 11 provoked a rush to the altar and, for us, the renewed popularity of rings inscribed with romantic sentiments.

'Creating trends is important and we are working on a range of designs from the classic to the eccentric – diamond solitaires in beautiful textured settings, to layers of gypsy charms cascading across the body. Our collection constantly evolves our distinctive signature, always relevant to the vagaries of fashion.

'We work mainly within the discipline of hand technology and craftsmanship: employment of the lost-wax casting method of Ancient Egypt determines the materials used like sterling silver, 18-carat gold and platinum, and ensures the quality we desire for textured and engraved surfaces. Vitreous glass enamelling is an intrinsic part of the Wright & Teague collection. We have worked in many media, but now concentrate on gold, silver, platinum and precious and semi-precious stones.

'The next few seasons will see oversized African inspired graphic pieces in softest yellow gold. Both vintage and tribal themes are trends that will continue strongly; also, inscription jewellery with more meaningful and poetic sentiments is becoming popular. Being the originators of the latter, this pleases us greatly.'

For more about Wright & Teague, go to www.wrightandteague.com

SWANKY MODES YOUNG IDE
CARRIAGES AT THREE BARE [
KOKO EVA THE CROSS VANII
PAMPAS KOKON TO ZAI LYN>
THE GLASSHOUSE SADIE THI
PUSSY GALORE ANANYA GA
RITA VALPIANI CONCRETE CC
MATCHES THE WEST VILLAGE
SWEET DREAMS CRUISE DUI
FLUIDITY MALAPA SHOON D
RELLIK SUNDAY BEST GEESE
JEANNE PETIT FOOTLIGHTS
THE CROSS BLUE LAGOON H

CLUE THE CHANGING ROOM
ERSE SIXTY SIX BODY BASICS
THE HAMBLEDON BROWSE
AMICA PANACHE FLANNELS
RA LADY ATTICA N.SHELLEY
O OYSTER GOTHAM ANGELS
ICHE BEAU MONDE VERDICT
ICHMOND CLASSICS SEFTON
ICH TRADER CAROLINE BLAIR
ERSE **DIRECTORY** WARDROBE
HE HOUSE MADELEINE ANNE
NE YOUNG POPPY BERNARD
O BOHO TCS POPPY INDIGO

DIRECTORY

South-east England

Ananya
4 Montpellier Street, London, SW7 1EZ
020 7584 8040

Anna
126 Regent's Park Road, Primrose Hill,
London, NW1 8XL
020 7483 0411

Anne Furbank
41 High Street, Buckden,
St. Neots, PE19 5WZ
01480 811 333

Bare
8 Chiltern Street, London, W1U 7PU
020 7486 7779

Base
55 Monmouth Street, Covent Garden,
London, WC2H 9DG
020 7240 8914

Bernard
4–6 High Street, Esher, Surrey, KT10 9RT
01372 464 604

Boho
113a Northcote Road, London, SW11 6PW
020 7924 7295

Celia Loe
68 South Molton Street, London, W1K 5ST
020 7409 1627

The Changing Room
10a Gees Court, Saint Christopher's Place, London, W1U 1JL
020 7408 1596

Concrete
35a Marshall Street, London, W1F 7EX
020 7434 4546

Courtyard
5–6 Angelgate, Guildlford, Surrey, GU1 4AN
01483 452825

The Cross
141 Portland Road, London, W11 4LR
020 7727 6760

Diverse
294 Upper Street, London, N1 2TU
020 7359 8877

The Dulwich Trader
9 Croxted Road, London, SE21 8SZ
020 8761 3457

Ego
102–104 Watling Street, Radlett,
Hertfordshire, WD7 7AB
01923 852 843

Envy
51 High Street, Cobham, Surrey, KT11 3DP
01932 863 484

Eva
12 High Street, Ipswich, IP1 3JX
01473 236 650

Fluidity
43 Bell Street, Henley-on-Thames,
Oxfordshire, RG9 2BA
01491 412 323

Footlights
21 Oakdene Parade, Cobham, Surrey, KT11 2LR
01932 860 190

The Glasshouse
15 East Street, Brighton, East Sussex, BN1 1HP
01273 326 141

South-east England

Gotham Angels
23 Essex Road, Islington Green, London, N1 8DU
020 7359 8090

Guilio
5–7 Sussex Street, Cambridge, Cambridgeshire, CB1 1PA
01223 316 166

Hero
3 Green Street, Cambridge, CB2 3JU
01223 328 740

Indigo
1–2 Baffins Lane, Chichester, West Sussex, PO19 1UA
01243 789 099

Jeanne Petitt
3 Bridge Street, Hungerford, Berkshire, RG17 OEH
01488 682472

Joy
432 Coldharbour Lane, Brixton,
London, SW9 8LG
020 7787 9616

Kokon to Zai
57 Greek Street, London, W1D 3DX
020 74341316

Malapa
41 Clerkenwell Road, London, EC1M 5RS
020 7490 5229

Matches
13 Hill Street, Richmond, Surrey, TW9 1FX
020 8332 9733

N. Shelley
75–79 High Street, Billericay, Essex, CM12 9AS
01277 621 000

Rellik
8 Golborne Road, London, W10 5NW
020 8962 0089

Sefton
271 Upper Street, London, N1 2UQ
020 7226 9822

Shop 77
77 Queens Road, Buckhurst Hill, Essex, IG9 5BW
020 8505 5111

Sixty 6
66 Marylebone High Street, London, W1U 5JF
020 7224 6066

Sweet Dreams
6 High Street, Cornwall Place, Buckingham, MK18 1NT
01280 812 507

TCS
28 High Street, Teddington, Middlesex, TW11 8EW
020 8977 8492

Vanilla
13 South Parade, Summertown, Oxford, OX2 7JN
01865 552 155

Walkers of Pottergate
25 Pottergate, Norwich, Norfolk, NR2 1DX
01603 618 718

Wardrobe
42 Conduit Street, London, W1S 2YH
020 7494 1131

The West Village
35 Kensington Park Road, London, W11 2EU
020 7243 6912

Willma
339 Portobello Road, London, W10 5SA
020 8960 7296

South-west England and Wales

L'amica
14 Post Office Road, Bournemouth, BH1 1BA
01202 780 033

Bishop Phillpotts
Quay Street, Truro, Cornwall, TR1 2HE
01872 261 750

Body Basics
79 Pontcanna Street, Cardiff, CF11 9HS
029 2039 7025

The Hambledon
10 The Square, Winchester, SO23 9ES
01962 890 005

Hollyhock
25–27 New Street, Salisbury, SP1 2PH
01722 411 051

JAQ
16 Margaret's Buildings, Bath, BA1 2LP
01225 447 975

Pussy Galore
18 High Street Arcade, Cardiff, CF10 1BB
029 2031 2400

Richmond Classics
Yelverton Road, Bournemouth, BH1 1DF
01202 295 298

Shoon
14 Old Bond Street, Bath, BA1 1BP
01225 480 095

Square
4–7 Shires Yard, Milsom Street, Bath, BA1 1BZ
01225 464 997

Square Spots
70a Eastgate, Cowbridge, South Wales, CF71 7AB
01446 773 776

Willy's
24 Gandy Street, Exeter, EX4 3LS
01392 256 010

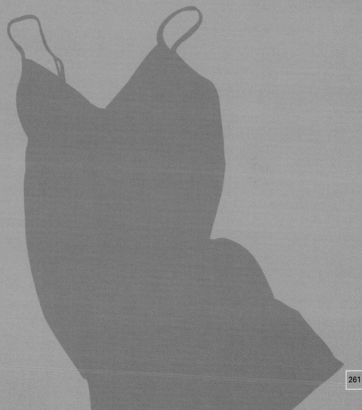

Midlands

Carriages at Three
3 The Wool Market, Cirencester,
Gloucestershire, GL7 2PR
01285 651 760

Jane Young
7/10 Chain Lane, Newark, NG24 1AU
01636 703 511

Katherine Draisey
58 Drury Lane, Solihull, B91 3BH
0121 704 2233

Madeleine Ann
45 Drury Lane, Solihull, B91 3BP
0121 704 9454

Scotney's for Women
132 London Road, Leicester, LE2 1EB
0116 255 9261

Young Ideas
St. John Street, Ashbourne, Derbyshire, DE6 1GP
01335 342 095

North England

Arc
Smithfield Building, 59 Oldham Street, Northern Quarter,
Manchester, M1 1JR
0161 831 7454

Attica
2 Old George Yard, Cloth Market,
Newcastle upon Tyne, NE1 1EZ
0191 261 4062

Bal Harbour
55 Bury Old Road, Prestwich, Manchester, M25 0FG
0161 773 5554

Beau Monde
2 The Weir, Hessle, Hull, HU13 0RU
01482 644 605

Blue Lagoon
46 London Road, Alderley Edge,
Cheshire, SK9 7DZ
01625 583 107

Browse
42 King Street, Whalley, Clitheroe, Lancashire, BB7 2EU
01200 426293

Caroline Blair
10 Library Road, Kendal, Cumbria, LA9 4QB
01539 730 500

Drome Couture
14 Cavern Walks, Liverpool, L2 6RE
0151 255 0525

Flannels
68–78 Vicar Lane, Leeds, LS1 7JH
0113 245 5229

North England

Garbo
Altringham Road, Wilmslow, Cheshire, SK9 5NN
01625 521 212

Geese
74 Bridge Street, Manchester, Lancashire, M3 2RJ
0161 839 3921

The House
69 High Street, Yarm,
Stockton-on-Tees, TS15 9BH
01642 790 816

Lynx
20 West Park, Harrogate, HG1 1BJ
01423 521 404

Morgan
15 Watergate Street, Chester, CH1 2LB
01244 347 717

Morgan Clare
3 Montpellier Gardens, Harrogate, HG1 2TF
01423 565 709

Oyster
1 Booth Street, Manchester, M2 4DU
0161 839 7575

Pastiche
7 & 9 Old Bank Street, Manchester, M1 7PE
0161 832 8595

Pollyanna
14–16 Market Hill, Barnsley,
South Yorkshire, S70 2QE
01226 291 665

Poppy
17–18 Market Square, Lytham, St. Anne's,
Lancashire, FY8 5LW
01253 730 826

North England

Rita Valpiani
50a–54 Parliament Street, Harrogate, HG1 2RL
01423 523 644

Sadie the Bra Lady
62 Front Street, Consett, Co. Durham, DH8 5AL
01207 503 032

Sunday Best
Victoria Jubilee Buildings, Bank Street, Rawtenstall
Rossendale, Lancashire, BB4 8DY
01706 215 495

Tessuti
14–20 Watergate Street, Chester, CH1 2LA
01244 400 055

Van Mildert
19–21 Elvet Bridge, Durham, DH1 3AA
0191 384 8500

DIRECTORY

Scotland

Clue
45 Thistle Street, Edinburgh, EH2 1DY
0131 220 6174

Corniche
2–4 Jeffery Street, Edinburgh, EH1 1DT
0131 556 3707

Cruise
180–188 Ingram Street, Glasgow, G1 1DN
0141 572 3232

Jane Davidson
52 Thistle Street, Edinburgh, EH2 1EN
0131 225 3280

Kafka
5 Alford Place, Aberdeen, AB10 1NP
01224 626 002

Moon
10 Ruthven Lane, Glasgow G12 9BG
0141 339 2315

Pampas
78/80 Hyndland Road, Glasgow, G12 9UT
0141 339 8860

Swanky Modes
49 Rose Street, Aberdeen, AB10 1UB
01224 624 950

Verdict
13 Thistle Street, Aberdeen, AB10 1XZ
01224 644 558

Zoomp
2–6 Jopps Lane, Aberdeen, AB25 1BR
01224 642 152

Carter Clothing
11 Upper Queen Street, Belfast
Co. Antrim, BT1 6LS
02890 243 412

The Glasshouse
3 Bedford House, Bedford Street
Belfast, BT2 7FD
02890 312 964

Koko
613 Lisburn Road, Belfast, BT9 7GT
02890 687 797

Panache
723 Lisburn Road, Belfast, BT9 7GU
02890 382 796

BREAKTHROUGH BREAST CANCER

Breakthrough Breast Cancer is a charity dedicated to fighting breast cancer through research and awareness, and has established the UK's first dedicated breast-cancer research centre, in partnership with the Institute of Cancer Research. Breakthrough's scientific work ultimately aims to eradicate breast cancer by discovering the causes of the disease, finding methods of prevention and developing new treatments, with results being translated as quickly as possible into practical help for patients.

Breakthrough has brought together thousands of ordinary people with the fashion and beauty industries, the music industry and the comedy industry to tackle the serious issue of breast cancer.

For further information on Breakthrough's research work or ways to help raise funds please call 020 7405 5111 or visit www.breakthrough.org.uk

breakthrough
breast cancer

With the valued support of

AVON

partners for 10 years

Statistics

Breast cancer is the number-one health concern for women in the UK. More than 39,000 women are diagnosed with the disease each year – a rate equivalent to one woman diagnosed every fifteen minutes. The disease is still the biggest killer of women in this country, with 1,000 women dying every month.

Be breast aware

Nine out of ten breast lumps are not cancerous. However, it is important to have a GP check any unusual breast lumps as early detection of any cancer greatly increases a woman's chances of survival.

What can I do? Check your breasts. Do this by looking and feeling in any way that makes you feel most comfortable – in the bath, shower, when dressing, standing or lying down.

Learning how your breasts feel will help you know what is normal for you. There is no need to follow any particular routine, just be aware of any changes in your breasts.

Changes to look out for

Any change in the outline or shape of the breast, especially those caused by arm movements, or by lifting the breasts; any puckering or dimpling of the skin;

Lumps, thickening or bumpy areas in a breast or armpit that seem to be different from the same part of the other breast and armpit, especially if they have only

recently appeared; nipple discharge, new to you and not milky; bleeding or moist reddish areas that don't heal easily; any change in nipple position; a rash on or around the nipple.

Breast screening

Currently routine screening is offered to all women aged 50–64, with plans to extend this to those up to 69 from 2004. If you are in this age group, make sure you attend your screening appointments. If you are over 69, you can request to be screened.

Please encourage all female family members and friends over the age of 50 to go for breast screening.

Useful contacts

The following organisations and charities provide information and support to those affeted by breast cancer.

Breast Cancer Care
24-hour helpline: 0800 800 6000
Information: 020 7384 2984
Website: www.breastcancercare.org.uk

CancerBACUP
Information: 0808 800 1234
Councelling: 020 7696 9000
Website: www.cancerbacup.org.uk

Bristol Cancer Help Centre
Information: 0117 980 9505
Website: www.bristolcancerhelp.org.uk

KNOW YOUR STATUTORY RIGHTS

One of the pieces of information we have highlighted in each review is a shop's policy on returns. As you will see from reading individual entries, these can vary quite widely from shop to shop. Clearly, many traders have goodwill policies that go beyond your statutory rights, and some traders will exchange clothes because they are the wrong size or even because you have made a mistake about the style or colour. It's worth remembering that a returned item needs to be in pristine condition – that is, unworn and undamaged; independents in particular simply cannot afford to accept return of an expensive item if it cannot be resold.

Below is a guide to help you understand your statutory rights. These facts are set out by the Office of Fair Trading.

You have certain basic legal rights when you buy goods or services. These rights also apply to goods bought or hired from a shop, street market, mail-order catalogue or doorstep seller. They also include goods bought in a sale.

Goods must be of satisfactory quality. This covers the appearance and finish of the goods, their safety and their durability.

Goods must be free from defects, even minor ones except when they have been brought to your attention by the seller before payment took place.

Goods must be fit for their purpose. This means the goods must perform the function for which you have been told they are intended.

Goods must be as described on the package or display materials. If you are told a garment is 100% cotton, then it cannot turn out to be cotton and polyester.

Once you have noted that something is wrong, tell the seller as soon as possible. If you are unable to return to the shop within a few days of purchase, telephone your complaint and make a note of the conversation and to whom you spoke.

ACKNOWLEDGMENTS

Author's Acknowledgments

When I first set out to make this book, I assumed there would be all types of trade lists I could consult and make choices from these and other lists that must be held by organisations like the British Fashion Council and the Association of Independent Retailers. I was a little naïve.

Thanks must go to *Drapers Record* – my favourite trade read for help in tracking down entries father afield than my own stomping ground in – up until recently Hackney (where the splendid 'Red' and 'Helsinki' in Stoke Newington Church Street have met my needs for many years). Thanks also for to *Drapers Record* for the chance to advertise for entrants from their letters page and thanks especially to Sarah Nash at *Drapers Record* for all her time and effort.

Very special thanks, however, goes to Juliet Yashar who has visited every shop with a list of my retailing desires and standards. Her organisation, patience and methodical research as well as her sound judgement and informed opinion has made this book possible. There is diligence and then there is Juliet.

Thanks to Breakthrough Breast Cancer who allowed me to access women through their vast database and receive recommendations of 'off the beaten track independents' via e-mail.

I would also like to thank the retailers and shop managers who rose to this project, despite not knowing what it was at first. I would also like to thank the PRs I dealt with especially Jo at Purple and Filiz at Brower Lewis, Richard at Beverly Cable and Jane Galpin for speedy effectiveness.

Thanks also our designers and specialists who contributed their knowledge and vision to the Future Gazing section.

Thank you John Wilson at the British Fashion Council for sourcing figures on the number of clothing retailers in this country and for putting me in touch with the splendid Peter Cooper. And to Jasmin Eldoori, India Faulkener-Wiley and Lindsey Franklin.

Thank you to all the staff at Conran Octopus especially Lorraine Dickey and Katey Day. And a heartfelt thanks to Michael Johnson, Kath Tudball and Julia Woollams at Johnson Banks for the design of this book – never has there been such a colourful and stylish approach to directory design.

And thank you to Mateda and Roseby for never knocking on the office door during the last week of frenzied e-mailing and technological madness and finally thank you Anna for looking after my children while I could not.

Publisher's Acknowledgments

Conran Octopus would like to thank all contributing shops, designers and the following photographers and organisations for their kind permission to reproduce their images in this book. All images are pertinent at the time of going to press, but featured shops may change their stock and suppliers.

Every effort has been made to trace the copyright holders and we apologise in advance for any unintentional omission and would be pleased to insert the appropriate acknowledgement in any subsequent editions.

ACKNOWLEDGMENTS

2 Courtesy of Johnny Loves Rosie; 5 Dan Lecca/Beverley Cable PR (design: Matthew Williamson); 14–15 Courtesy of Halpern Assc.; 17 Kristina Haslund; 25 Tim Griffiths (design: Boyd); 26–27 Stephen Brown; 28–29 Russell Duncan; 34 Chris Moore (design: Gharani Strok); 44–45 Courtesy of Amanda Wakeley; 46–47 Hannah Tooke; 48–49 Courtesy of Agar Studios; 54–55 Courtesy of Maverick PR; 58 Courtesy of Nicole Farhi AW02; 63 Courtesy of Lulu Guinness; 64 Courtesy of Nick Lawes PR; 68–69 Paul Miller; 70 Courtesy of Brower Lewis PR (design: Jimmy Choo); 72 Lewis Gasson; 76 Courtesy of Nick Lawes PR; 78 Chris Moore (design: Dolce & Gabbana); 82–83 MCK Photography; 84–85 Andrew Lamb (design: Ghost); 86 Baker Evans; 88–89 Courtesy of Shirley Pinder; 98 Anthea Simms (design: Moschino); 100 Bob Berry; 102–103 Courtesy of Amanda Wakeley; 106–107 Courtesy of Flax PR (design: Fenn Wright & Manson); 114–115 Tim Mercer; 116 Andrew Lamb (design: Ghost); 118 Courtesy of Lulu Guinness; 119 Dan Lecca/Beverley Cable PR (design: Matthew Williamson); 121 Gerardo Somoza (design: DKNY); 124 Courtesy of Attire; 127 Courtesy of Philip Ingall & Assc.; 128 Chris Moore (design: Paul Smith); 131 Chris Moore (design: Kenzo); 132–133 Courtesy of Johnny Loves Rosie; 134 Gerardo Somoza (design: DKNY); 144 Anthea Simms (design: Versace); 146 Nick Roberts/ High Fashion (UK) Ltd (design: August Silks); 148–149 Tim Griffiths (design: Maria Grachvogel); 150 Courtesy of Betty Barclay; 156–157 Courtesy of Brower Lewis PR (design: Jimmy Choo); 158 Jeff Gilbert; 159 Chris Moore (design: Michiko Koshino); 162–163 In Camera Photography; 166 Andrew Lamb (design: Ghost); 168–169 Dan Lecca/Beverley Cable PR (design: Matthew Williamson); 170–171 Jeff Starley; 174 Chris Moore (design: Max Mara); 176–177 Courtesy of MDA International (design: Lauren Vidal); 178 Courtesy of Eveden Ltd (design: Rigby & Peller); 180 Chris Moore (design: Ghost); 184 Courtesy of Burberry; 190 I.W.M; 193 Chris Moore (design: Dolce & Gabbana); 194–195 Mairi Semple; 196–197 Courtesy of Burberry; 202–203 Graham Burkhill; 204 Courtesy of 1st Design (design: Paula Frani); 206 Andrew Lamb/Brower Lewis PR (design: Betty Jackson); 212 Chris Moore (design: Kenzo); 214–215 Phil Smyth; 216 Chris Moore (design: Dolce & Gabbana); 223 Joanna van Mulder; 224–225 Tony Hopewell/Getty Images; 226 Courtesy of Brower Lewis PR (design: Earl Jean); 228 Perry Curties (stylist: Charty Durrant); 231 Courtesy of Riverhouse Creative Consultants; 232 Courtesy of Georgina Goodman Ltd; 234 Courtesy of Purple PR; 237 artist: Rachel Wingfield; 238–239 Courtesy of Anya Hindmarch; 240 Geoffrey Clements/Corbis; 243 Paul Edmondson/Corbis; 244 Victor Boullet (design: Fabris Lane); 246 Mads Armgarrd (artist: Prof. Helen Storey); 249 Dan Lecca/Beverley Cable PR (design: Matthew Williamson); 250 Courtesy of Riverhouse Creative Consultants; 252 Martyn Thompson (design: Wright & Teague); 270 Lewis Gasson